d on or before
KT-407-512
HDRAWN
054479
THE HENLEY COLLEGE LIBRARY

images **26**

What goes on inside our heads is a wondrous thing.

Our brains turn lightwaves into shapes, associate colours with moods, recognise a face in a crowd, and can differentiate hats from pencils.

Neurologists have discovered that artists will have more highly developed brain cortex dedicated to the processing of visual information.

And since no two people have the same neuron routes the images retrieved from our consciousness will never be identical.

Images **26** is a collection of the very best neural collisions that occur inside the heads of some very special people – the illustrators.

Images 26 published by
The Association of Illustrators
81 Leonard Street
London EC2A 4QS
T +44 (0) 20 7613 4328
E info@a-o-illustrators.demon.co.uk
W www.aoi.co.uk
www.aoisupplement.co.uk

Book design
Atelier Works

ISBN 09515 448 45
Printed in China

Association of Illustrators
81 Leonard Street
London EC2A 4QS
T +44 (0)20 7613 4328
F +44 (0)20 7613 4417
E info@a-o-illustrators.demon.co.uk
W www.aoi.co.uk
www.aoisupplement.co.uk

Production in Hong Kong by
Hong Kong Graphics and Printing Ltd
T (852) 2976 0289
F (852) 2976 0292

Exhibitions and Events Manager
Harriet Booth
T +44 (0) 20 7739 8901

Membership and Publications Secretary
Anna Steinberg & Matt Johnson
T +44 (0) 20 7613 4328

Acknowledgments
We are grateful for the support of many organisations and individuals who contribute to the Images exhibition and annual as follows:

Our dedicated team of judges for applying their expertise to the difficult task of selecting this year's work

The Royal College of Art for hosting the Images 26 Exhibition

Pentagram Design Ltd for their kind support of Images 26 through The Pentagram Award

Matt Lee for the use of his illustrations in this annual

Russell Cobb for the use of his illustration on the Call for Entries form

Finers Stephens Innocent for their legal advice

Nicole Peli for the production of Images 26

Ian Chilvers and Alexandra Coe at Atelier Works for their design

Simon Yorke at Waterloo Wine Co

AOI Managing Council
Francis Blake, Michael Bramman, Derek Brazell, Stuart Briers, Joanne Davies, Leo Duff, Adam Graff, James Marsh, Sam Taylor, David Webster and Lawrence Zeegen

All our dedicated casual staff and volunteers for their invaluable assistance with the competition and exhibition

contents

about the AOI

The AOI was established in 1973 to advance and protect illustrator's rights and encourage professional standards. The AOI is a non-profit making trade association dedicated to its members' professional interests and the promotion of illustration.

Members consist primarily of freelance illustrators as well as agents, clients, students and lecturers. The AOI is run by an administrative staff responsible to a Council of Management.

As the only body to represent illustrators and campaign for their rights in the UK, the AOI has successfully increased the standing of illustration as a profession and improved the commercial and ethical conditions of employment for illustrators.

Campaigning
The AOI is a member of the British Copyright Council and the Creators Copyright Coalition. It helped set up the secondary rights arm of DACS, the UK visual arts collecting society.

The AOI was responsible for establishing the right of illustrators to retain ownership of their artwork and continues to campaign against loss of copyright control, bad contracts and exploitative practices. We will expose companies who consistently abuse illustrators' rights.

Information and support services

Portfolio Advice
Members are entitled to a free annual consultation with the AOI's portfolio consultant. Objective advice is given on portfolio presentation and content, suitable illustration markets and agents.

Journal
The AOI Journal is distributed bi-monthly to members, keeping them informed about exhibitions, competitions, campaigns and activities in the profession. Also available to non-members on subscription.

Hotline advice
Members have access to a special Hotline number if they need advice about pricing commissions, copyright and ethics problems.

Publications
The AOI publishes Rights: The Illustrator's Guide to Professional Practice, a comprehensive guide to the law for illustrators. It provides detailed advice on how to protect against exploitative practices and contains a model contract for illustrators to use. We also produce Survive: The Illustrator's Guide to a Professional Career which is a comprehensive practical guide to beginning and continuing a career as a professional illustrator. Survive includes information about marketing, ethics, agents and a guide to fees. These publications are available to members at reduced rates.

Client Directories
The AOI currently has three illustration client directories. The Editorial Directory has details of over 120 contacts in the newspaper and magazine industries. The Publishing Directory is a comprehensive list of over 150 important contacts in book publishing. The Advertising Directory has details of over 150 contacts from the world of advertising.

Business advice
Members are entitled to a free consultation with the AOI Chartered Accountant, who can advise on accounting, National Insurance, tax, VAT and book-keeping.

Regional groups
The contact details of regional representatives are available to members who organise social activities for regional members and provide an important support network.

Discounts
Members receive discounts on a range of services, including a number of art material suppliers nationwide.

Legal advice
Full members receive advice on ethics and contractual problems, copyright and moral right disputes.

Return of artwork stickers
Available to AOI members only. These stickers help safeguard the return of artwork.

Students and new illustrators
Our seminars and events, combined with the many services we offer, can provide practical support to illustrators in the early stages of their career.

Events
The AOI runs an annual programme of events which include one day seminars and evening lectures. These include talks by leading illustrators as well as representatives from all areas of the illustration field, and cover such subjects as children's book illustration, aspects of professional practice, new technologies and illustrators' agents. AOI members are entitled to discounted tickets. To request further information or a membership application form please telephone +44 (0)20 7613 4328

Website
Visit our website at www.aoisupplement.co.uk for details of the Association's activities, including samples from current and past journals, details of forthcoming events, the AOI's history and on-line portfolios.

Patrons
Glen Baxter
Peter Blake
Quentin Blake
Raymond Briggs
Chloe Cheese
Carolyn Gowdy
Brian Grimwood
John Hegarty
David Hughes
Shirley Hughes
Sue Huntley
Mick Inkpen
Donna Muir
Ian Pollock
Gary Powell
Tony Ross
Ronald Searle
Paul Slater
Ralph Steadman
Simon Stern
Peter Till
Janet Woolley

foreword

Michael Bramman

Chair

What people say about Images…

"I used to devour old AOI annuals when I was at college in Australia in the early 80's. So for me Images has a real history that I'm proud to be part of."
Shane Mc Gowan,
Illustrator

"For reference, for inspiration and for finding the right illustrators fast – Images is the book we use."
Tom Reynolds,
Design Director,
The Sunday Times Magazine

As its first major venture in self publishing, Images 26 is another landmark in the history of the Association of Illustrators. Again designed by Atelier Works, we have enlisted the services of Nicole Peli on production, co-ordinated by Events Manager Harriet Booth and supported by the AOI staff and Council.

In keeping with the AOI's policy of student advancement the designers were briefed to select one of the student entrants to illustrate the category dividers and portraits of the judges. This has been splendidly accomplished by Matt Lee from University of Plymouth in Exeter.

For this year's competition the judges were sent a CD of the work entered in their category, thus eliminating the problem of losing any of those chosen who wouldn't be able to attend on any given day, which meant a wider selection of judges were available to us.

As the only British source book where the work is judged by established and respected artists and designers, Images has consistently been the book that commissioners refer to and which enjoys a long shelf life. Following the exhibition selected works will go on a national tour. The entire published editions of Images comprise the most prestigious archive of contemporary British illustration available today.

Images 26 is a fitting testimonial to the continued success of the AOI and the dedication and work of its staff, Council, subcommittees and those members who have donated their time and expertise along with the support of our Patrons.

Since the last Images exhibition there has been a noticeable increase in the AOI's fortunes and activities. The seminars and events have had an enthusiastic response. The lottery proved to be both a popular event and fundraiser. Last April's AGM saw the biggest attendance for some years. So we must be doing something right.

We have been working with the SAA and Association of Photographers on issues of copyright and we look forward to the possibility of a joint exhibition with the AOP. We have reaffirmed links with the New York Society of Illustrators with honorary membership conferred on both chairs and an increase in mutual information. A programme to encourage the practice of good drawing as the basis of illustration in the art college curriculum has also been instigated. I have noticed a series of articles in the press recently deploring the standard of drawing among young contemporary artists. A situation, I'm pleased to note, not in evidence among the work exhibited in Images 26.

Once again we are pleased to be holding the exhibition at the Royal College of Art and we welcome the return of the Pentagram Gallery Award.

My congratulations both to this year's award winners and all successful entrants, and to those who didn't make it, better luck next time.

Success to you all.

Michael Bramman
Chair

some of my best friends...

Lynn Trickett

20 November 2001

There is an old, apocryphal story about the graphic designer who tries to explain to his mother what he does. He is particularly proud of a new brochure and so he decides to show it to her.

She says;

"Very nice dear. Did you draw the pictures?"

"No"

"Did you write the words?"

"No"

"Did you take the photographs?"

"No"

"Well what did you do?"

I suspect that the reason I have been invited to write this introduction is not for my Mum, but as a commissioner of illustration. I love illustration. Some of my best friends are illustrators. I can't draw – but I know what I like! There, I've admitted to every 'designer cliché'. Now I can try to explain why I think designers and illustrators should learn to love each other again.

It is the relationship between Designer and Illustrator which is key. To start with, it has to be a relationship between equals. That obviously works both ways. I don't want to think of you as a 'supplier' and you don't want to think of me as 'the enemy'!

For us, the most satisfying projects start with a dialogue, initially between Designer and Client, then between Designer, Illustrator, Writer and Client at different or sometimes the same time. Sounds chaotic, but it is our job to orchestrate it, to facilitate the process and filter out the parts that need only go to one recipient. All our clients are different. Some love to be involved at every point. Others prefer to be more removed. The same applies to the illustrators that we work with. Some like to be told exactly what to do, others would do anything to avoid being predictable. It is our job to know how to choose the right person for a particular job; how to work with different personalities and to bring out the best in them.

We certainly don't consider our clients are 'the enemy' and we want to avoid our chosen illustrator feeling that they are. Sometimes it is easier said than done and I would be lying if I said we had never had a problem in the thirty years of Trickett & Webb. But not often, thank goodness. It all comes back to dialogue. You need to keep up a three way communication to get to the best results.

In the 'olden days', back in the first half of the twentieth century, there wasn't really the same problem. Illustrators and designers were all rolled into one 'Commercial Artist'. Abram Games and Tom Eckersley worked hard at a dialogue with their client, but they didn't require a third person in the equation. They would have been outraged to think that they needed someone else to deal with the type on a poster – and even more outraged to be given someone else's concept to work to.

Then along came the big divide. Art Schools began to appeal to a much wider range of kids and, eventually, divided into more specialist areas. Illustration and Graphic Design were no longer part of the same thing. As Graphic Design became more of a sexy destination for school kids, the two departments became ever more separated within art schools.

It has now got to such an extreme that to try to set up a joint project, where designers and illustrators work together, is almost impossible. How short sighted is that? Surely, college is an ideal place for illustrators to begin to experience being art directed and for designers to test their skills at briefing and working with other equal professionals. We are not Fine Artists, working to our own agenda, and we have to develop our skills in working as a team. You could even call it a 'transferable skill' in these days of impossibly large year groups within both disciplines.

New technology has, in some cases, brought us back full circle to the all in one Commercial Artist. Graphic designers have felt much more confident in providing the whole 'package' for a client, creating their own imagery, whether by manipulation of available material or typographically. Sometimes the quality is there, more often it is not. Equally, colleges like RCA are breaking down the barriers so that many of their image-makers are as much designers as illustrators, with no fear of type or the written word.

All this depends on the quality of the individual. In some cases results are great – but it can often lead to a lowering of standards. In my view, there is no substitute for the coming together of a team of first class designer, image-maker and client – each adding their considerable skills. Why should I expect to be able to produce an image that is as wonderful as one by a professional chosen specially for the job – and why should an illustrator be able to design a piece of communication as well as I could?

Obviously different projects require different illustrators. Sometimes we will know exactly what we are looking for and the brief will be extremely tight. Other times we will be looking for the unexpected piece of 'magic' that we know our chosen illustrator is capable of. Every project has a 'tone of voice', which needs to be found. I am most interested in illustration with a distinct 'tone of voice'. I want to be able to look at an illustration and know who did it – or want to know who did it. Not for me the 'Wallpaper' style of illustration which could have been done by one of a string of people.

Although in the last decade, photographers have achieved far greater individuality in their work, it is still often hard to detect a unique 'tone of voice'. Illustrators are so lucky. Not only can they naturally produce individuality just by the way they make marks but they are unhampered by reality. They have the scope to be 'conceptual' and it is that kind of illustration, which interests me most.

For the past twenty-two years Trickett & Webb has produced a calendar as a joint collaborative with Augustus Martin, a screen-printing company and a changing group of illustrators. Other similar calendars have followed, but I am proud to say that we were probably the first. It was born of necessity. Augustus Martin asked us to design a calendar, but we knew that they would not want to pay for it! It needed to demonstrate how wonderful screen-printing can be, so it needed lots of imagery.

We set up a system where no money changes hands. We all work for free and get paid in calendars, which are sent to our best clients, press and friends. There are only a thousand copies produced, so it is very much a limited edition. Over the years it has gained a unique reputation – and has won a huge number of awards for illustration, design and print.

It is an opportunity for us to design something no client would pay for, for the illustrators to try out new ideas or techniques and for the printers to demonstrate that they can print more than 4p off posters! Being screen printed, it also smells great!

Each year we think of a theme, which often relates to words or word games. This year we chose 'oxymora', which are phrases or pairs of words with conflicting meanings; 'deliberate mistake' or 'full of holes'. We invited our group of illustrators to pick one from a list – and illustrate it. Only limitation is to use four colours and to provide separated artwork. Some times the younger illustrators have never done separated artwork. We always like to go through the process very carefully with each illustrator and we use previous calendars to demonstrate what is achievable in screen process rather than litho.

Very occasionally we have a problem with an illustration. For many years we thought that we could not 'reject' an image, because we were not paying for it. This meant that there was nearly always one image that we were less than happy with. Then a couple of the regular contributors told us that they thought we really should reject if it was necessary. Perhaps they felt secure that it was not going to happen to them! Anyway, the result was that we were more honest. We treated the calendar in the same way that we would have for a client. The result has been that we have always managed to sort things out, get an illustration we and the illustrator are happy with – and keep friends at the end of it! Oh and the 'regular contributors' have also had to make changes on occasion, but it has all been part of a friendly dialogue!

How has illustration changed over the twenty two year life of the calendar? Well the roughs are not as good! We used to get wonderful colour roughs that were sometimes better than the end job. Now we mostly get a scribble! That is OK though, because it comes as part of a dialogue so that we are all confident that we know what we will end up with. You can usually explain an idea with a simple drawing – and all our illustrations are idea based. I think that many of the early calendar illustrations are as good today as they were then, because a good idea has a much longer life than a piece of styling.

For our twentieth calendar, which coincided with the millennium, we persuaded Augustus Martin to let us design a fifty-three week calendar, which was called 'Week Link'. We wrote a fifty-three word statement, cut up the words and put them in a mug. Then we drew one word out for each illustrator.

It is, to me, an enduring example of the wonderful and quirky nature of illustrators that, out of fifty three, not one blanched at the idea of illustrating a single word – not even the ones that got 'in' or 'the'.

My best friends!

Advertising

Jason Brooks
Illustrator

Tony Chambers
GQ Magazine

Sarah Madge
Art Buyer, St Lukes

Peter Grundy
Illustrator

Ellie Rudolph
Art Editor, Money Observer

Editorial

Linda Boyle
Art Director,
You Magazine

Peter Davies
Illustrator

Marian Hill
Illustrator

Mark Porter
Creative Director,
The Guardian

Steve Thorogood
Thorogood Illustration

Books

David Bailey
Avenue Press

Suzanne Dean
Art Director CCV,
Random House

Maggie Hodgetts
Head of Graphic Design,
Waitrose Ltd

James Hood
Illustrator

Satoshi Kambayashi
Illustrator

Children's Books

Mandy Cleeve
Creative Head,
BBC Children's Books

Sandra Perry
Design Manager,
BBC Children's Books

Kathryn Coates
Deputy Head of Design,
The Times Supplements

Julie Monks
Illustrator

Jonathan Roberts
Design Manager,
Lion Publishing Plc

Nancy Tolford
Illustrator

New Media

Sarah Ellis
Creative Director,
Platypus Design Ltd

Michael Munday
Illustrator

Robert Mason
Illustrator, lecturer, writer

Harry Lyon-Smith
Illustration Ltd

Jason Simmons
Art Editor, MacUser

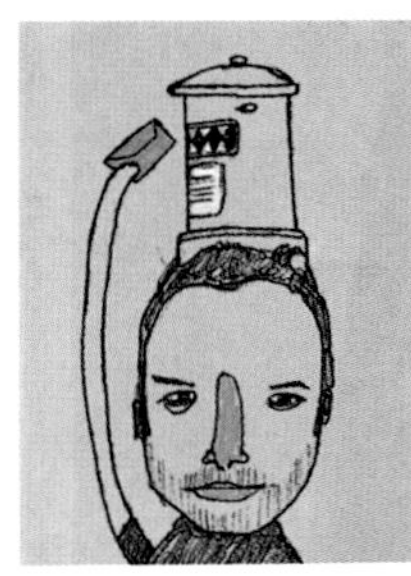

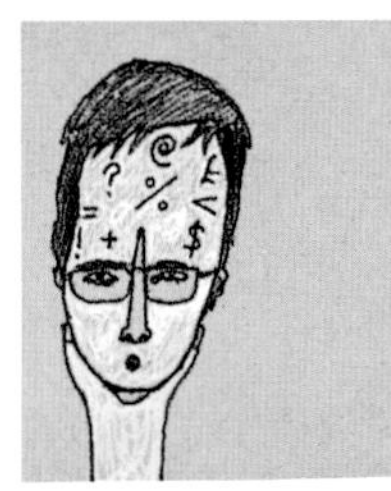

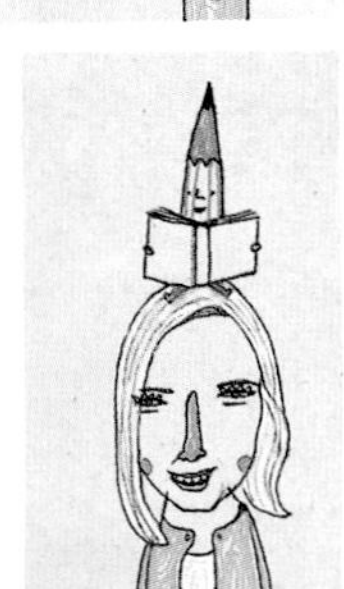

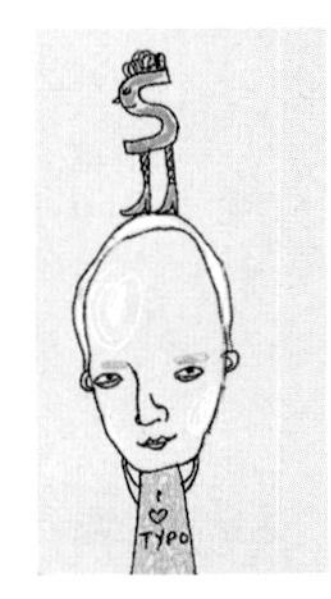

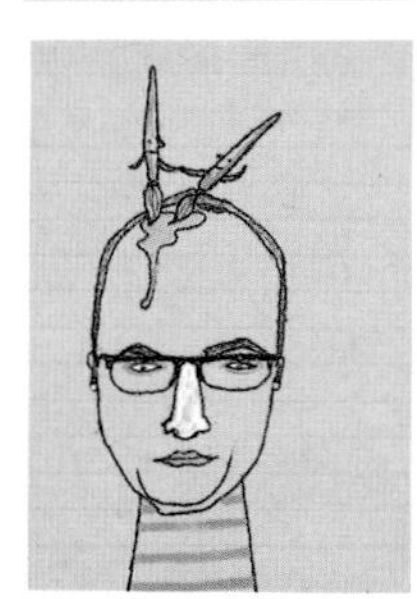

judges of **images**

Design

Mark Moran
Illustrator

Ali Pellatt
Illustrator

Jo Samways
Art Editor,
Oxford University Press

Stuart Steventon
Director, Rocket Design

Lynn Trickett
Designer/Director,
Trickett & Webb

Student

Russell Cobb
Illustrator

Leo Duff
Course Director
MA Drawing as Process,
Kingston University

Kate Elkin
Art Director,
Cosmopolitan

Joanne Hayman
Illustrator

Imran Mirza
The Right Stuff

Unpublished

Stuart Briers
Illustrator

Russell Mills
Artist/Illustrator

David Pearce
Tatham Pearce Design

Stephen Reid
Deputy Design Director,
Sunday Times Magazine

David Rooney
Illustrator

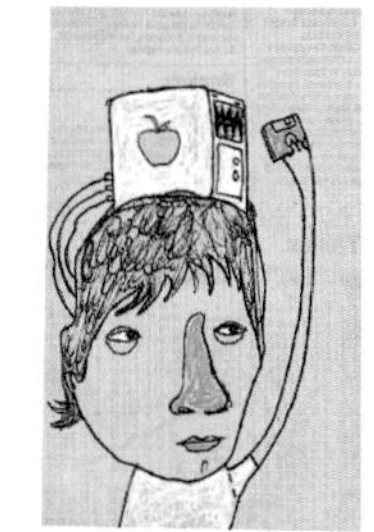

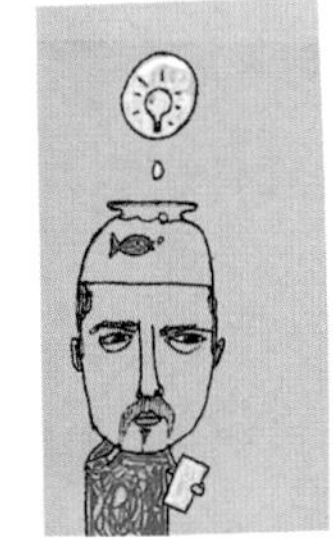

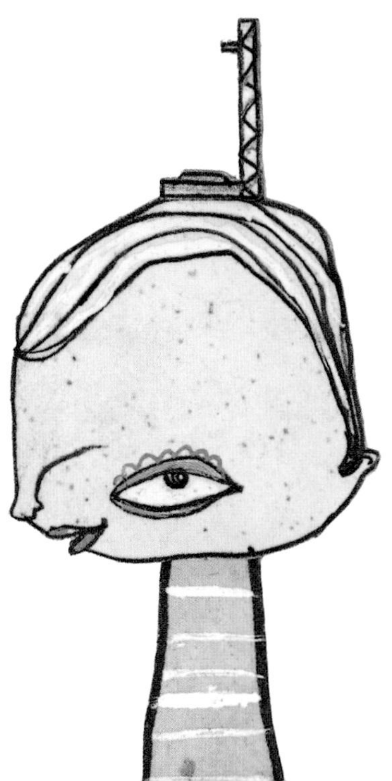

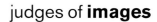

About the illustrations

M Medium
B Brief
C Commissioned by
F Firm

Awards

G Gold

S Silver

B Bronze

advertising **images**

Advertising
Gold award winner

Peter Grundy

G BT Internet

M Digital

B Create a simple character

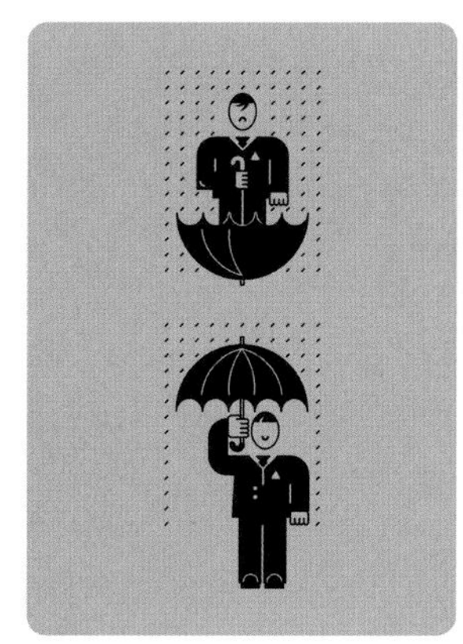

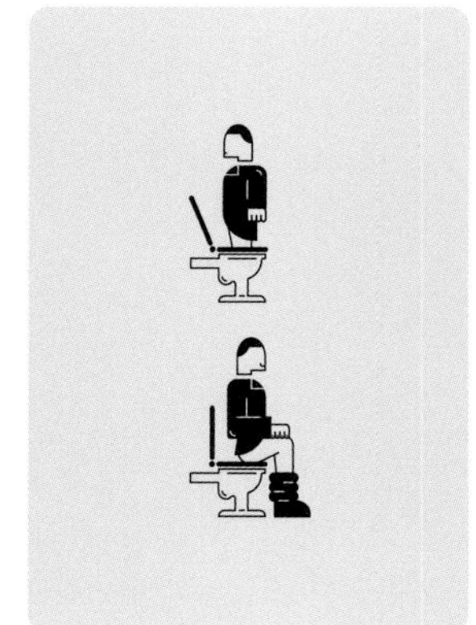

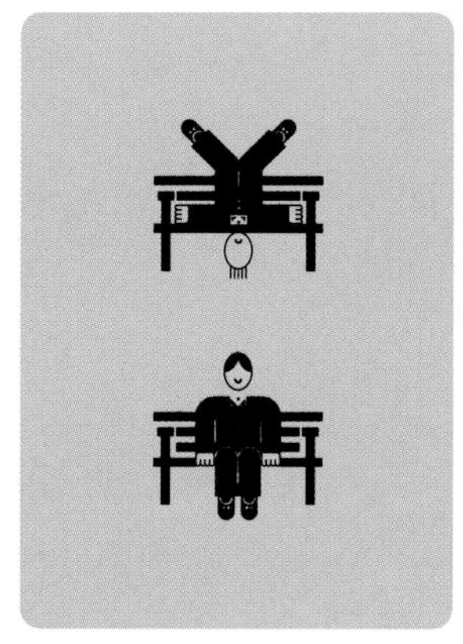

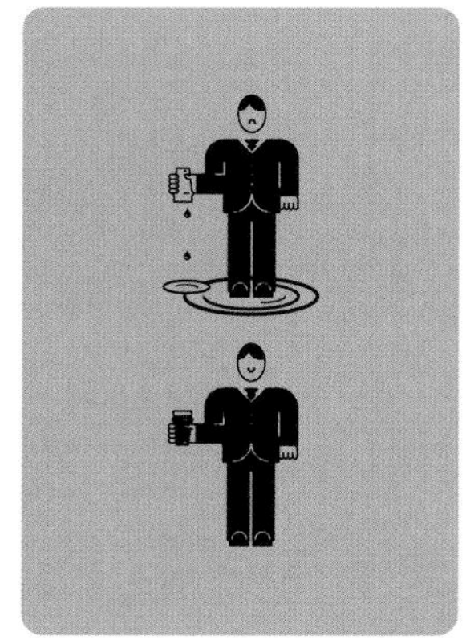

G

C Amanda Goonetilleke

F Abbott Mead Vickers

Paul Bateman
Rome

M Digital collage

B A montage to depict Rome, to promote it as a travel destination for users of the 'G.P.Platinum Card'

C Ben Dakin

F Haymarket Publishing

Syd Brak
Sexy Beast

M Movie poster

B Symbolising a typical London gangster enjoying life on the Costa del Sol, featuring the star of the film

C Paul Wilson

F Empire Design

Andrew Bylo
Wimbledon 2000

M Watercolour, gouache

B Aerial view of Wimbledon grounds to show Centre and no.1 courts

C John Davies

F Freelance designer (for All England Lawn Tennis Club, Wimbledon)

Graham Carter
Burn in Hell
M Original art / digital
B One of a series of ads for the 'Beware of the Voices' campaign

BEWARE OF THE VOICES. For career advice worth listening to and thousands of jobs, visit

F Saatchi & Saatchi / monster.co.uk

Russell Cobb
Southcorp Wines – Devils Lair

M Acrylic

B To create a fresh identity for Southcorp Wines combining history, region and typography

Peter Cox / Louis King
Anatomical Man

M Digital

B Designed for Schroders to advertise their Medical ISA in a national press campaign

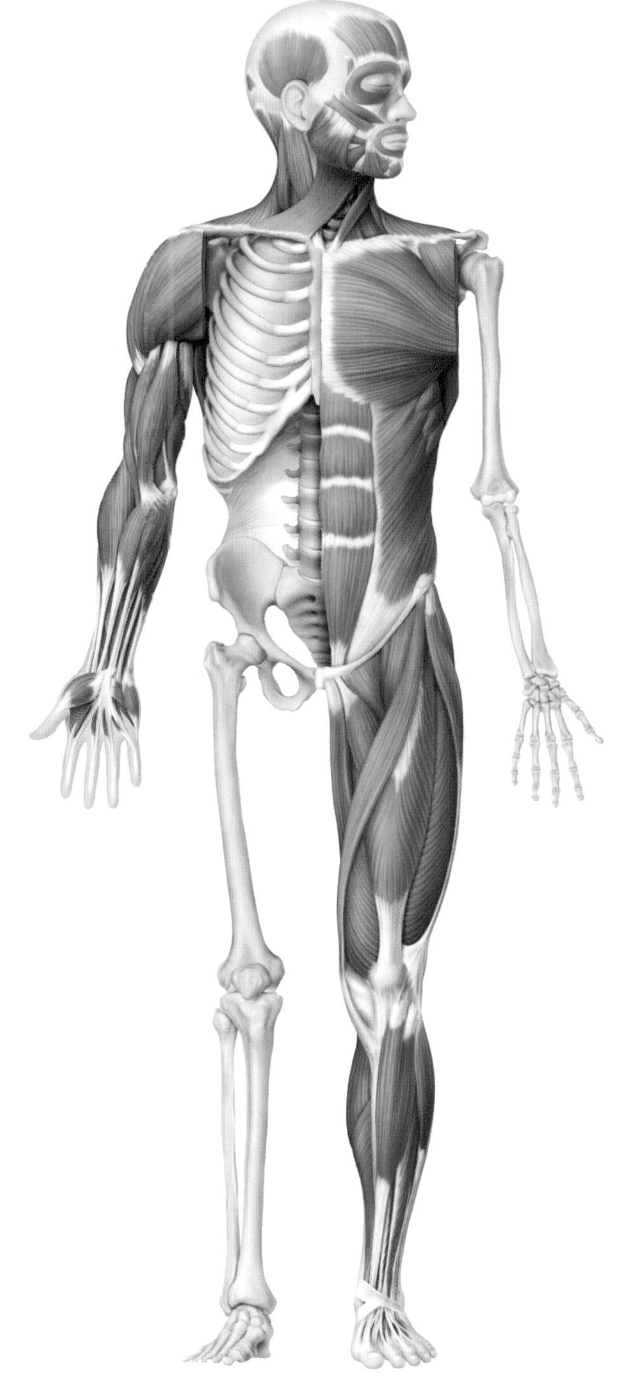

C Mark Reddy

F BMP DDB Needham (for Southcorp Wines)

C Tony Snow

F Rapier Ltd (for Schroders)

Carl Flint
Shark – Nestlé
Milky Bar Choo
Dinosaur – Nestlé
Milky Bar Choo

M Mixed media

B To use a combination of images to create an amusing advert with plenty of attitude that would appeal to 7-8 year olds

C Sharon O'Connell

F Lowe

Craig Frazier/Folio

(B) Lakeview

M Digital

B Illustration used to promote Ciana Book Fair

Matilda Harrison

upmystreet.com

M Acrylic

B An open brief to devise a picture which contained many hidden and visible elements that described the website's services

(B)

C Robert Collie

F Sandpiper Books Ltd

C Guy Moore

F Malcolm Moore Deakin

Paul Hess
upmystreet.com

M Watercolour

B An open brief to devise a picture which contained many visible and hidden elements that described the website's services

Steve May
Arenaworks.com

M Flash and Photoshop

B To visually interpret 'arenaworks' to advertise Arena's website

C Guy Moore

F Malcolm Moore Deakin

C Tamlyn Francis

F Arena

Lydia Monks

S Lots of Animals

M Acrylic

B To remind people that the RSPCA deal with many animals, not just cats and dogs

Ray Nicklin

Thinking 'Banana'

M Digital

B Critical judgement & presentation: elements common to Fine, Graphic and Applied arts. Image used for Summer (degree) Show publicity

S

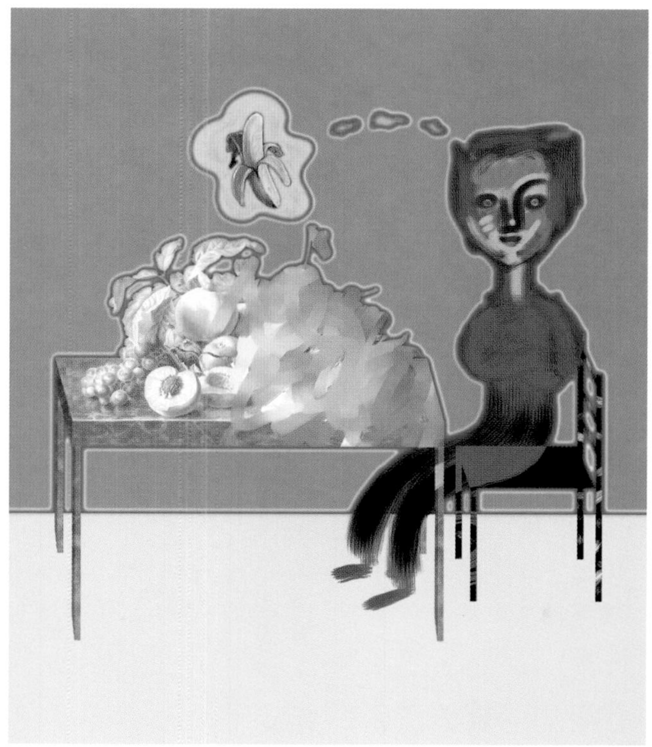

C David Dye

F Abbott Mead Vickers (for RSPCA)

C Steve Young

F Cardiff School of Art & Design

Maria Raymondsdotter
1/3 Off

M Mixed media

B To illustrate the student who can afford to visit all his girlfriends (1/3 off most rail fares)

C Leigh Roberts

F Craik Jones

Andy Smith
Hints of Bullshit
M Original art / digital
B Illustrate a wine drinking cow

F TBWA / Oddbins

Simon Spilsbury
Champions Mountain

M Mixed media

B To illustrate how champions league was a difficult mountain to climb, for press and POS

C Noel Hasson

F BHO/FCB (for Ladbrokes)

David Tazzyman
Sarah Couldn't Wait
M Original art / digital
B Drawing of a traumatised girl, upset because her mates are calling to tell her what a great time they're having

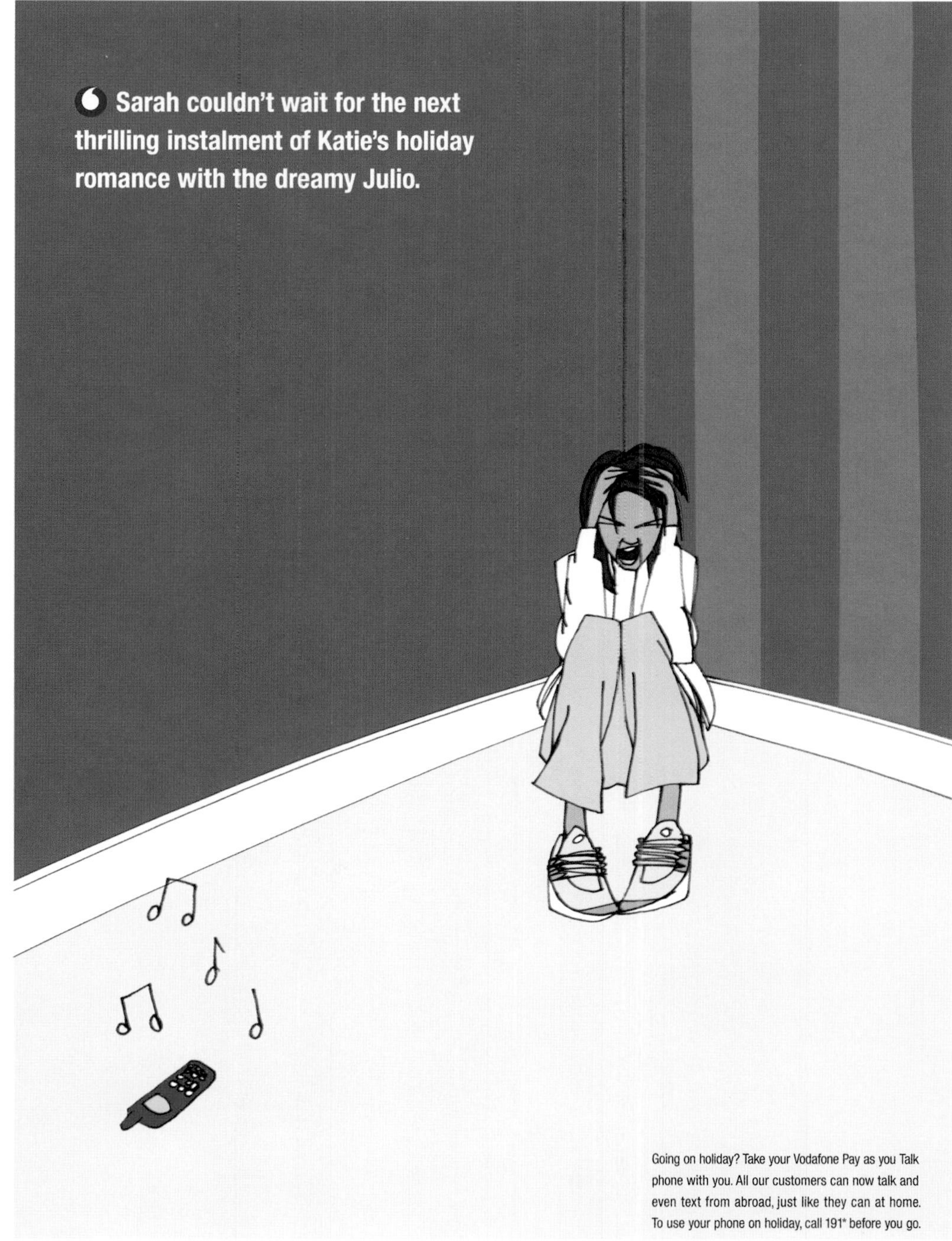

F WCRS

Bob Venables

Walkers Square Period

M Alkyd

B The agency required a painting for billboards in 'square period' style for Gary Lineker's launch of Walkers square crisps

The Glasswasher's Curse

M Alkyd

B A painting used as a prop in a photograph for a John Smiths beer billboard

C Mike Durban

F Abbott Mead Vickers (for Walkers)

C Clare Delafons

F TBWA (for John Smiths)

design and new media **images**
V

Design and new media
Gold award winner

Ian Whadcock
Damian Gascoigne
Picasso Pictures

G Switch to Powergen

M Digital

B Customer acquisition 30 second tv/cinema advertisement. A rabbit character in dream landscape – the world of Powergen – so easy to switch to Powergen you can do it in your sleep...

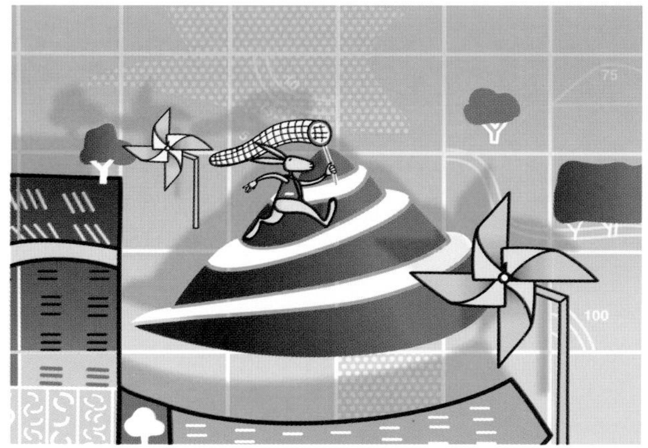

G

C Stuart Newman

F Miller Bainbridge & Partners (for Powergen Plc)

Andy Baker
Untitled 2
M Mixed media
B To illustrate the notion of 'At a Glance' for the Royal Mail website

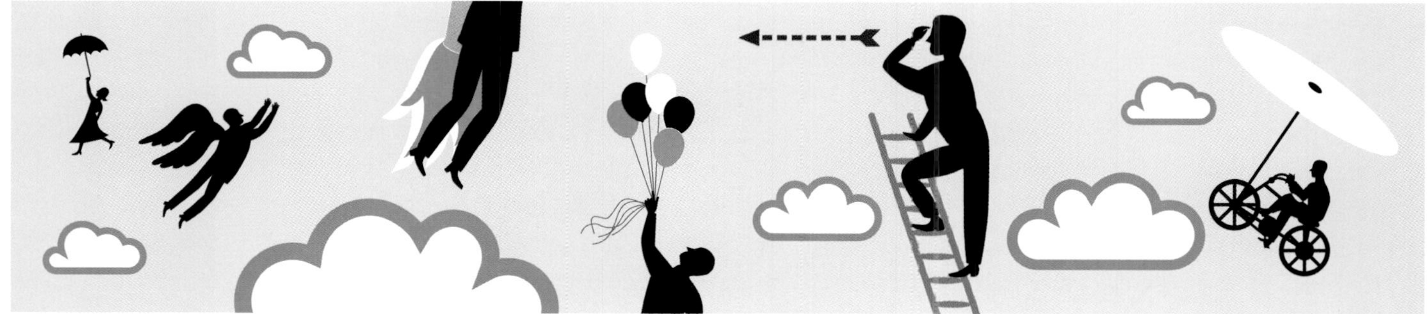

C Simon Thompson
F Rufus Leonard

Christine Farrell
Losing Your Train of Thought

M Linoprint

B Illustrate what it feels like to have aphasia – a communication impairment resulting from a brain injury. For publication, informing those who have acquired aphasia

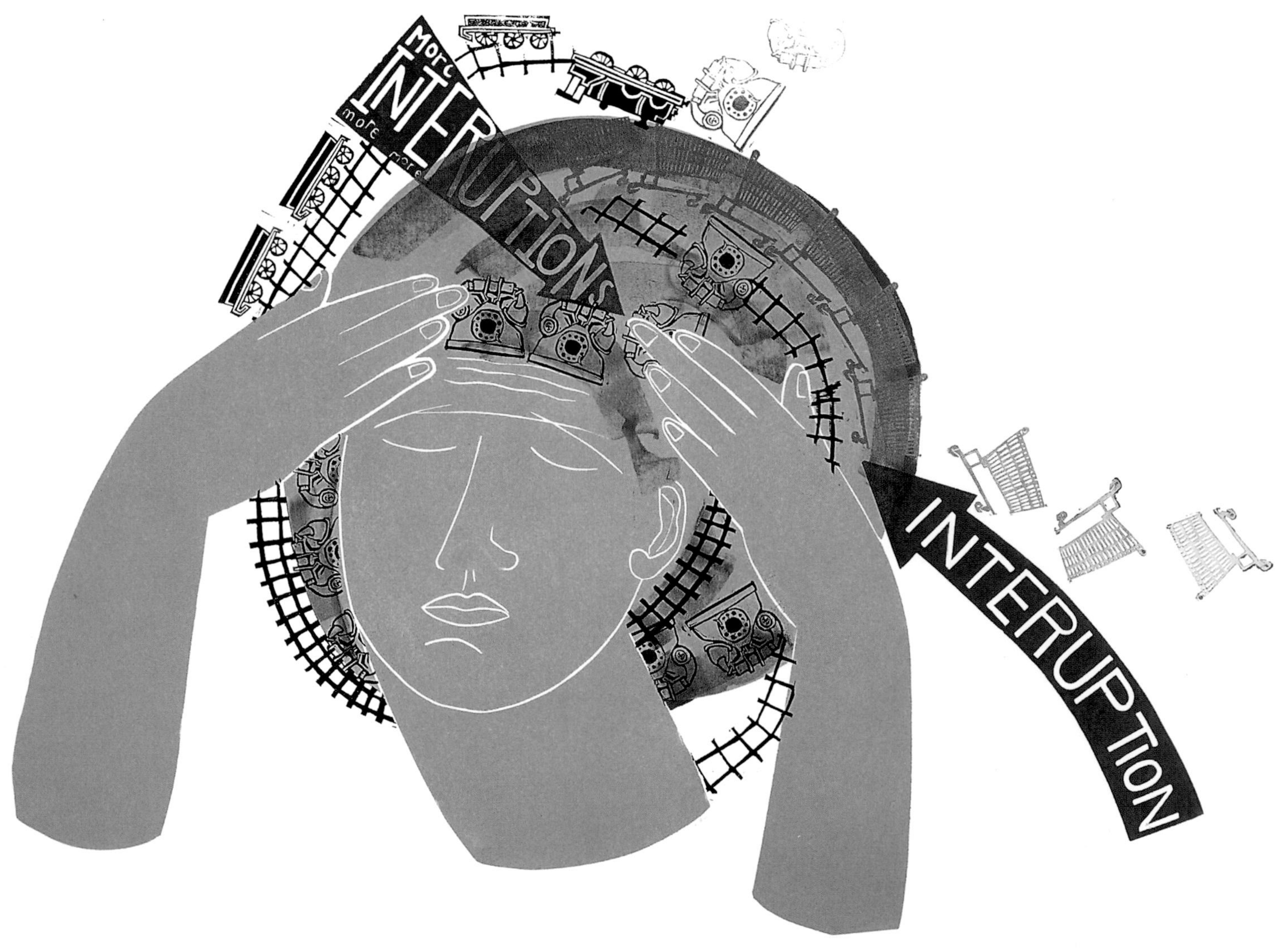

F Tayside Primary Care Trust

Tom Gauld
The Effect of
Original Thinking

M Gouache

B To depict the notion of original thinking in marketing

C David Freeman

F Enterprise IG (for WPP Group plc – Atticus Magazine)

Peter Grundy

City Won
City Too

City Free
City For

M Digital

B Create a set of images to go on the conference room wall at the new HQ of a Leicester company. The city theme reflects the work of Healey Chemicals

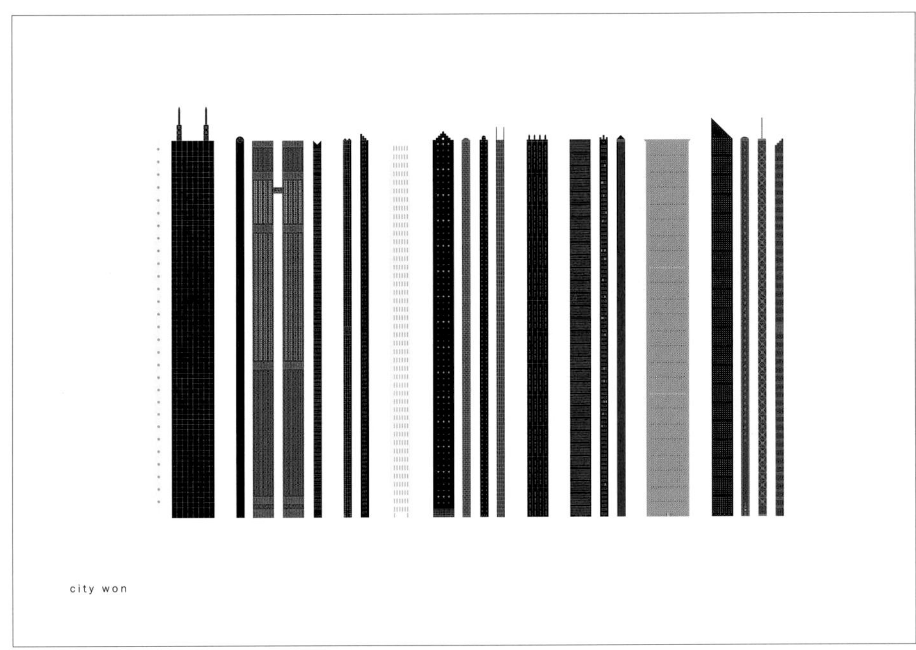

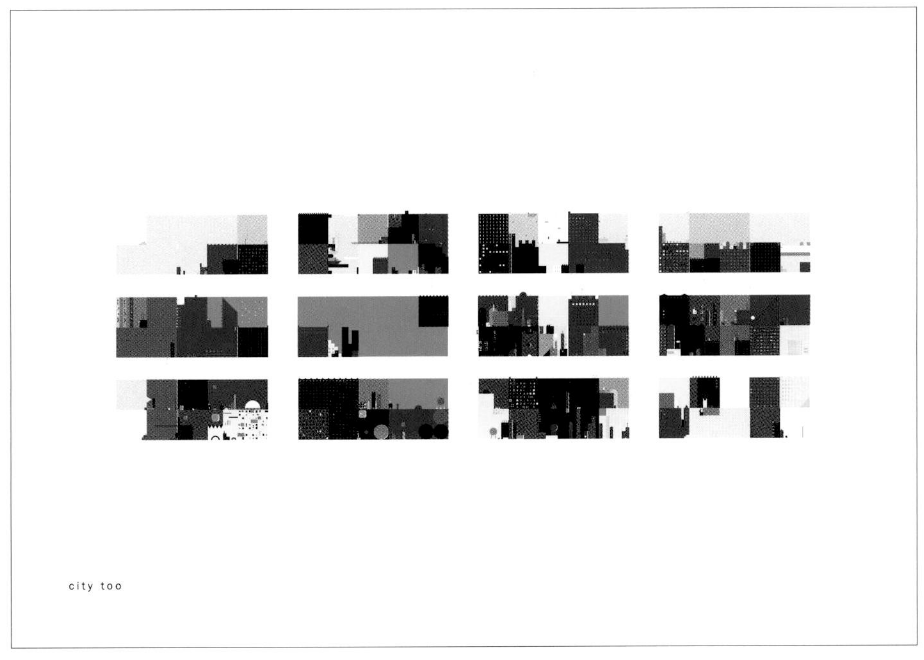

C Paul Atkinson

F Atkinson Design Associates (for Healey Chemicals)

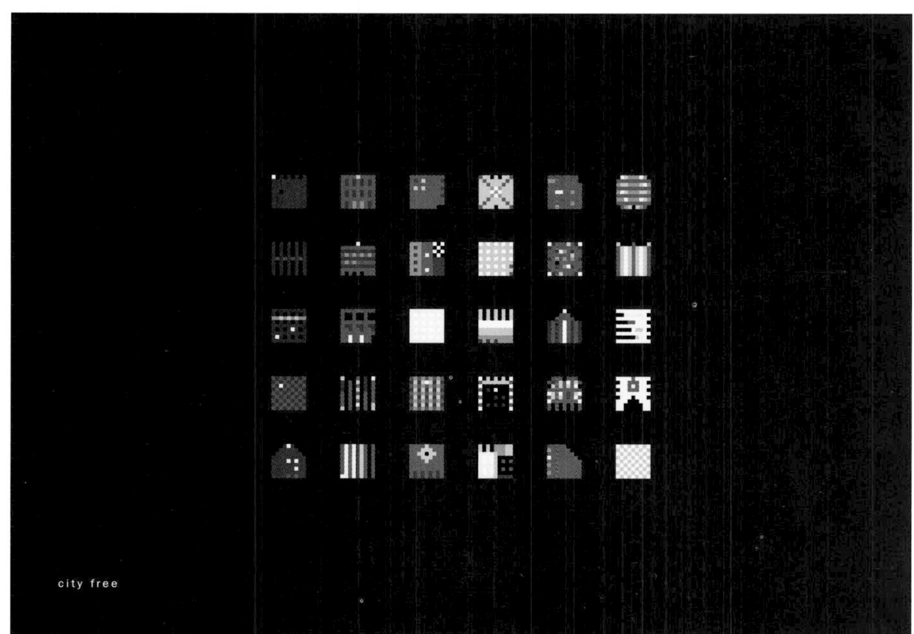
city free

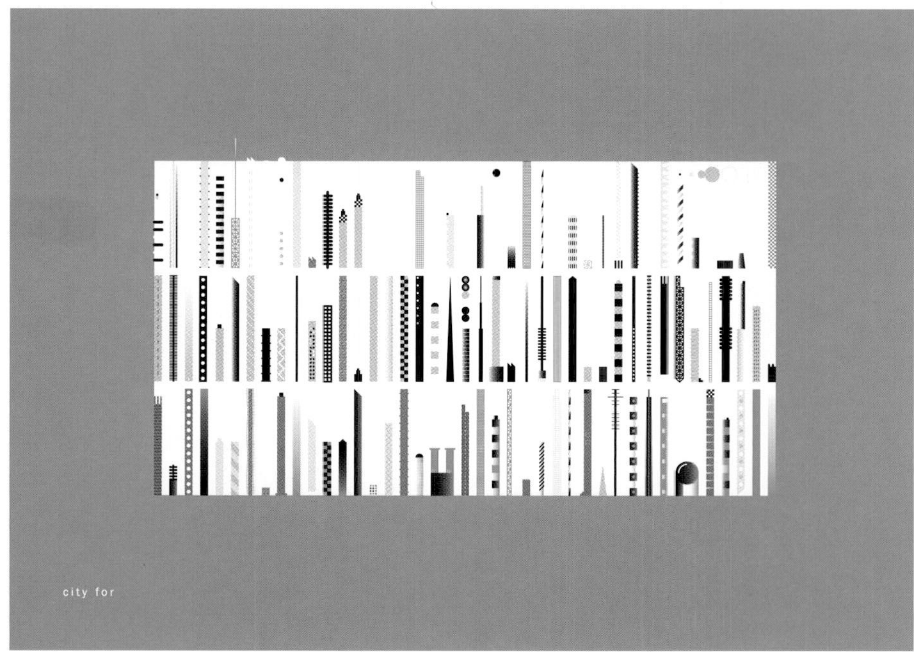
city for

Peter Grundy
Technique

M Digital

B Divider images for a book called 'Writing in the Digital Age'. Each image spells the action

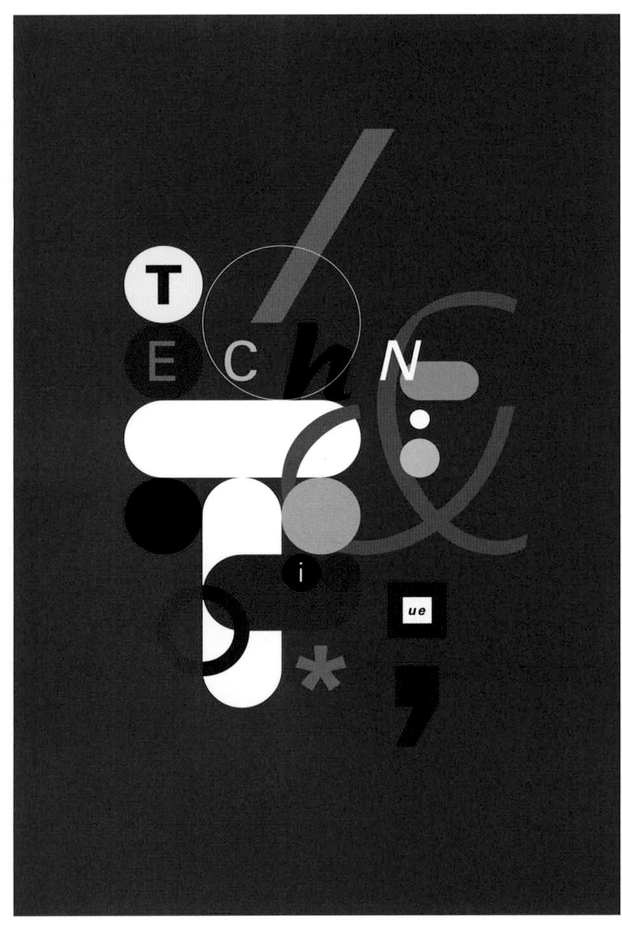

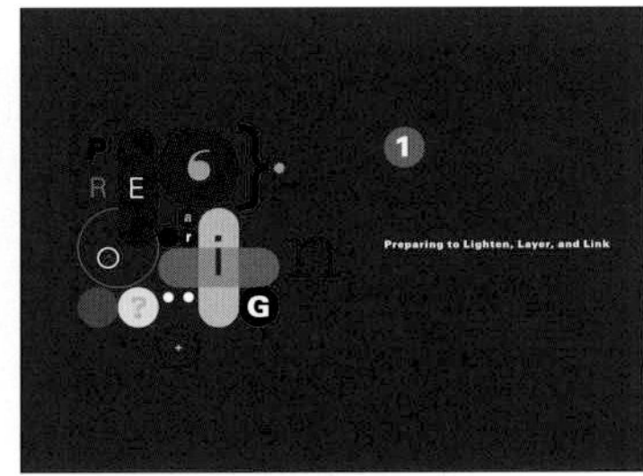

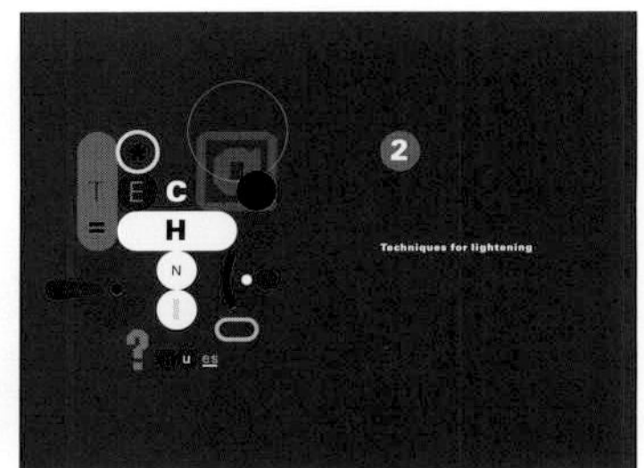

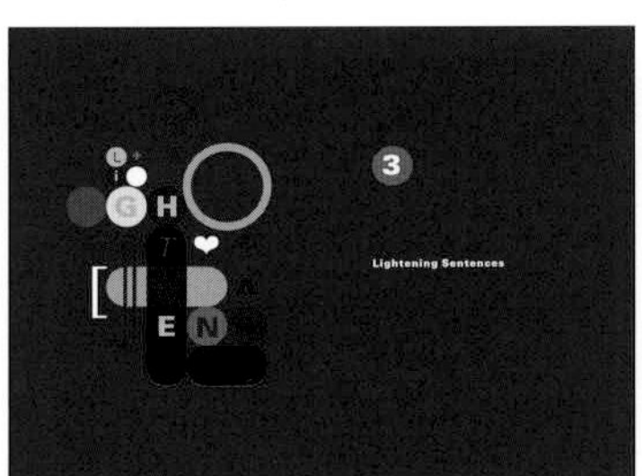

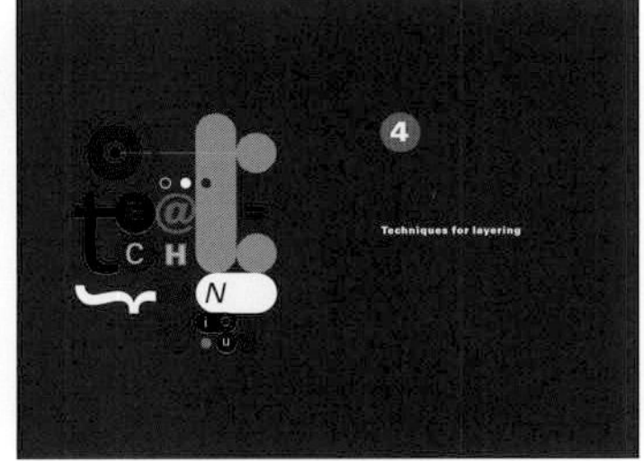

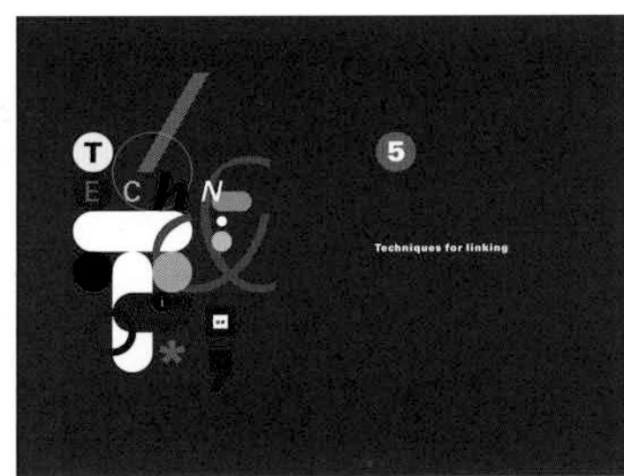

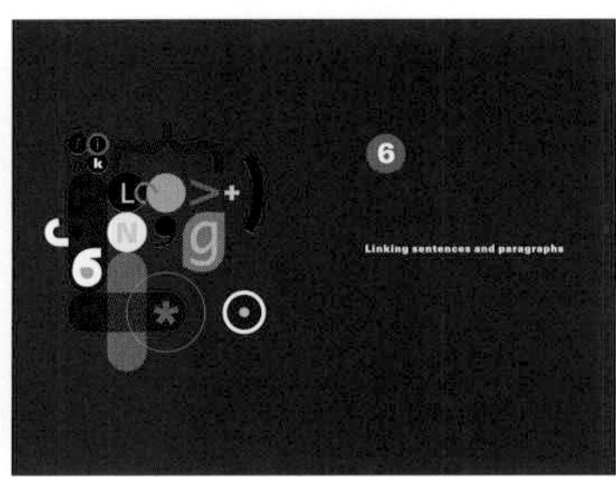

C Bruce Ross Larson

F CDI

Brent Hardy-Smith
Hallé for Youth logo
M Heat, thermal paper
B Produce a logo which playfully shows the four sections of an orchestra and also includes the conductor

Sara Hayward
Gate to the Sea
M Acrylic
B To produce an image for print capturing the atmosphere, colour, sunshine and warmth of a Mediterranean resort

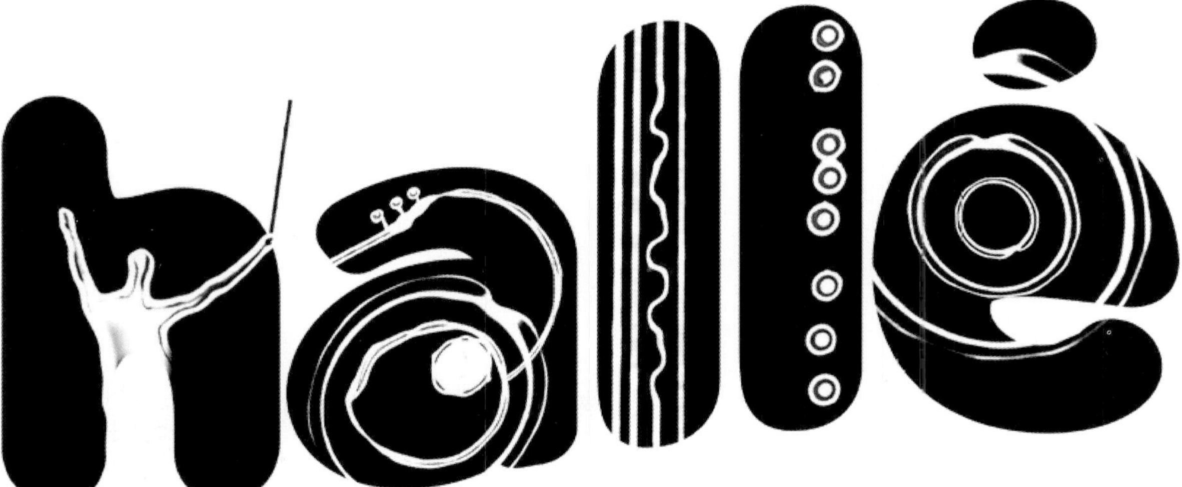

C Jo Bartlett
F Hallé Orchestra

C Lucy McDowell
F Felix Rosenstiel's Widow & Son

Lizzie Harper
Peacock Butterfly

M Watercolour

B Image of peacock butterfly for identification purposes; used on larger interpretation panel

Paul Hess
Gulliver's Travels

M Watercolour

B Inside annual report illustration to go over 4 pages, to show the size of the client's new printing machine

Yuko Hirosawa
I Hate Dog

M Ball point

B CD cover & 12 inch vinyl illustration for Dirty Vegas – line drawing

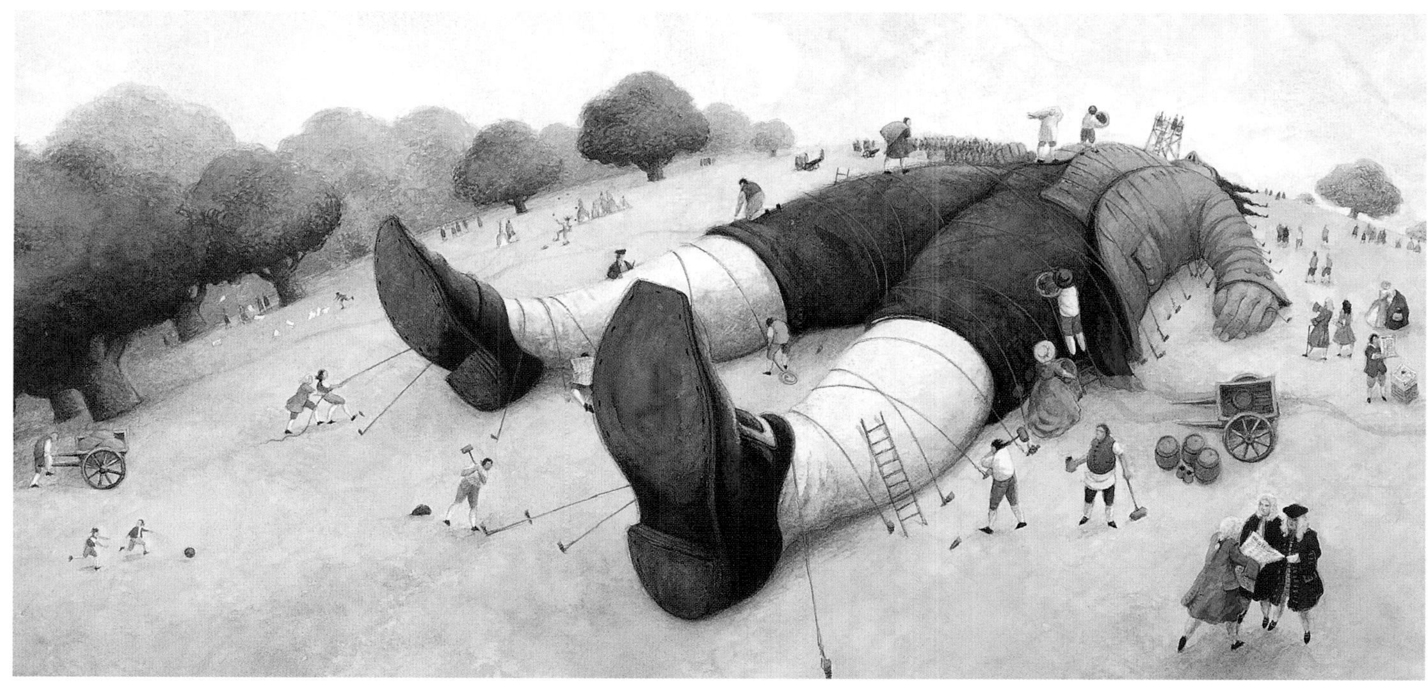

C Kerstin Haremsa

F Ogilvy and Mather (for Haindl Papier)

F Blue Source (for Dirty Vegas)

Peter Horridge

Merino

M Digital

B Produce an icon image of a Merino wool ram's head for the Woolmark Co. labelling of Australian Merino wool products

Tacchino

M Digital

B One of 6 pieces, each a different animal, for an Italian food producer used on packaging

C Sue Mould

F Elmwood (for Woolmark Co)

C Nina Fortune

F Identica (for Cappone)

Mick Marston

Pickling Trojans (a)

M Mixed media

B Self promotional piece, which includes poster and a CD-Rom containing games, animations, screensavers etc. Contact artist for CD.

Pickling Trojans (b)

M Mixed media

B Self promotional piece, which includes poster and a CD-Rom containing games, animations, screensavers etc. Contact artist for CD.

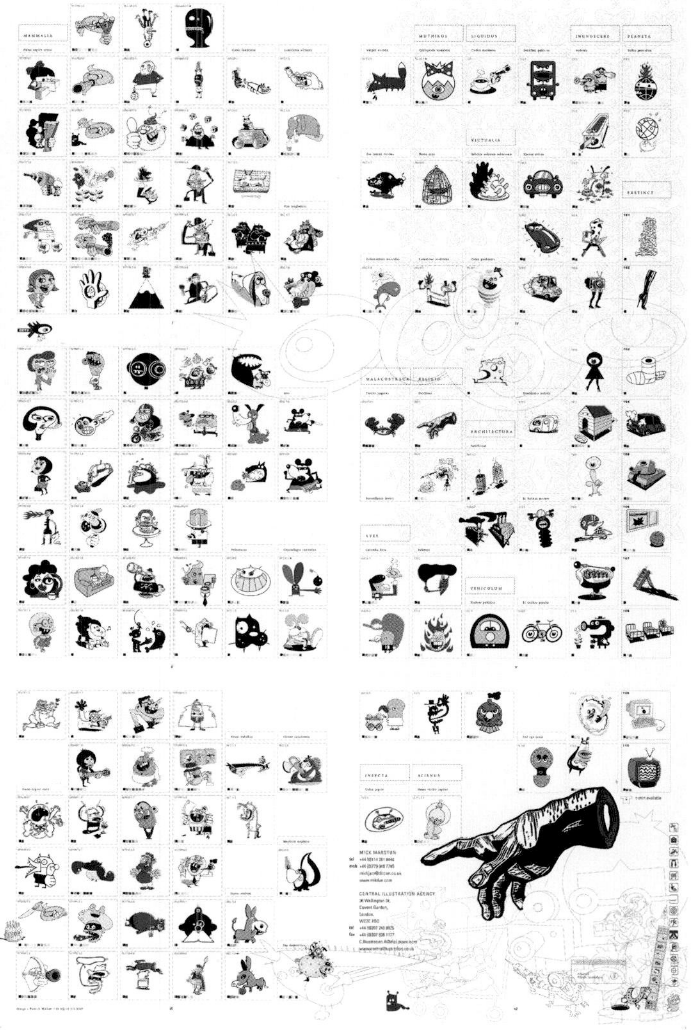

Steve May

S Gut (3) (2c)

M Flash and Aftereffects on Digibeta

B Still from final graduation film for MA at the RCA

S

Tony Meeuwissen
Weather

M Mixed media

B To produce a new format of four stamps which capture the humour and obsession we have with the weather in the UK

C Jane Ryan

F Royal Mail

Gunnlaug Moen Hembery
BaneTele
Annual Report

M Mixed media

B One of illustrations in the annual report for BaneTele (Norwegian Rail's telecommunication company). Illustrate the future and area of use in telecommunication for the railway. A series of illustrations and cover

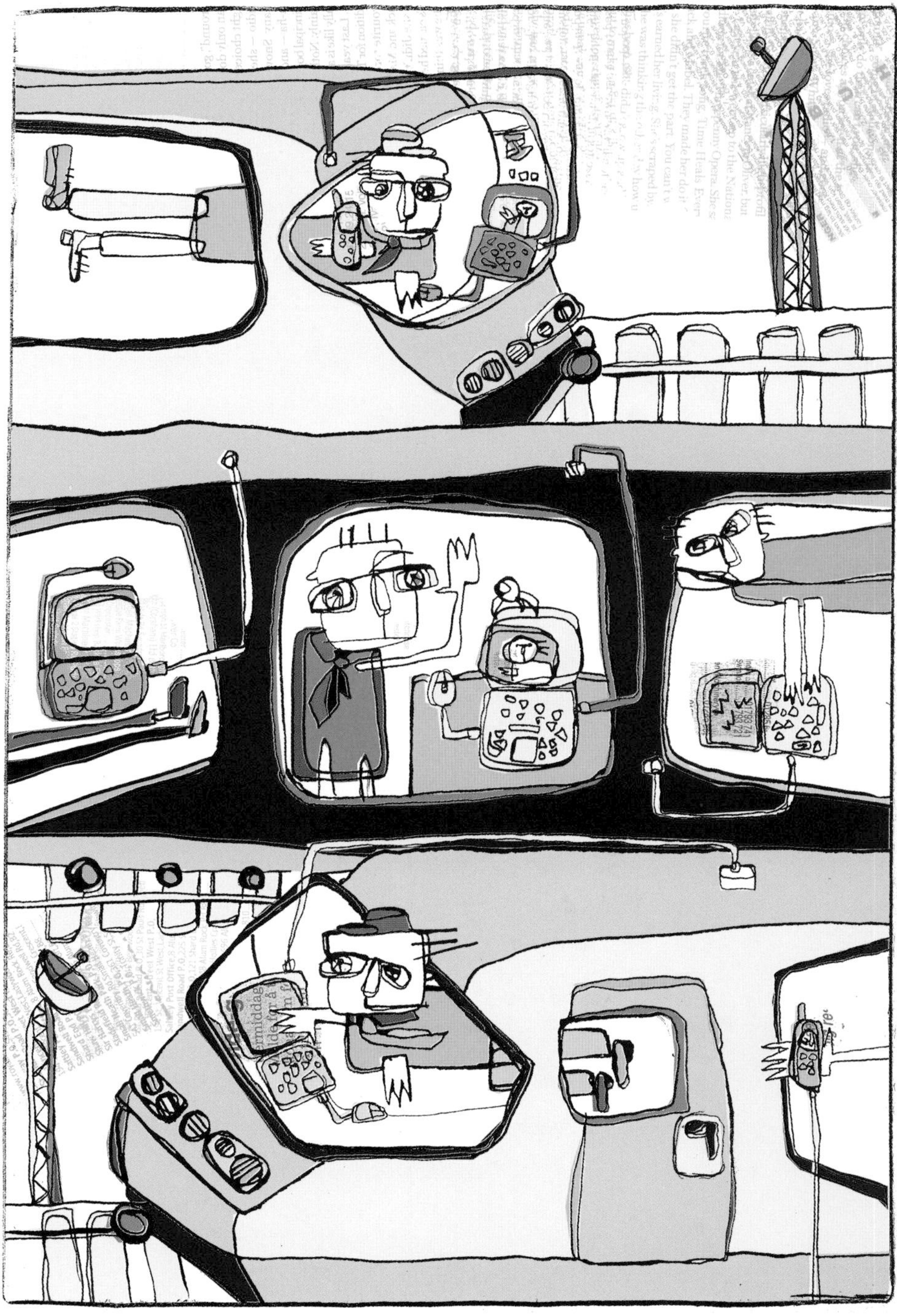

C Roy Nyvold

F Uniform

Julie Monks
Getting It Right
M Oils
B To illustrate McKinsey's Top Team Performance Brochure

C Michelle Thompson
F CDT Design (for McKinsey's)

Sarah Nayler
Art Gallery

M Line, digital

B Lots of people looking at floating blue sphere in art gallery instead of Old Masters, for annual report and website for financial company

Ian Murray
Magic City

M Digital, pen & ink

B Still from a Flash movie in which a man awakes to find himself in a magical city. Abstract forms and narrative content

C Michael Hirsch

F Pauffley (for Zurich Financial Services)

Tilly Northedge
Royal Festival Hall

M Digital

B The illustration is to show the location of the public spaces within the Royal Festival Hall

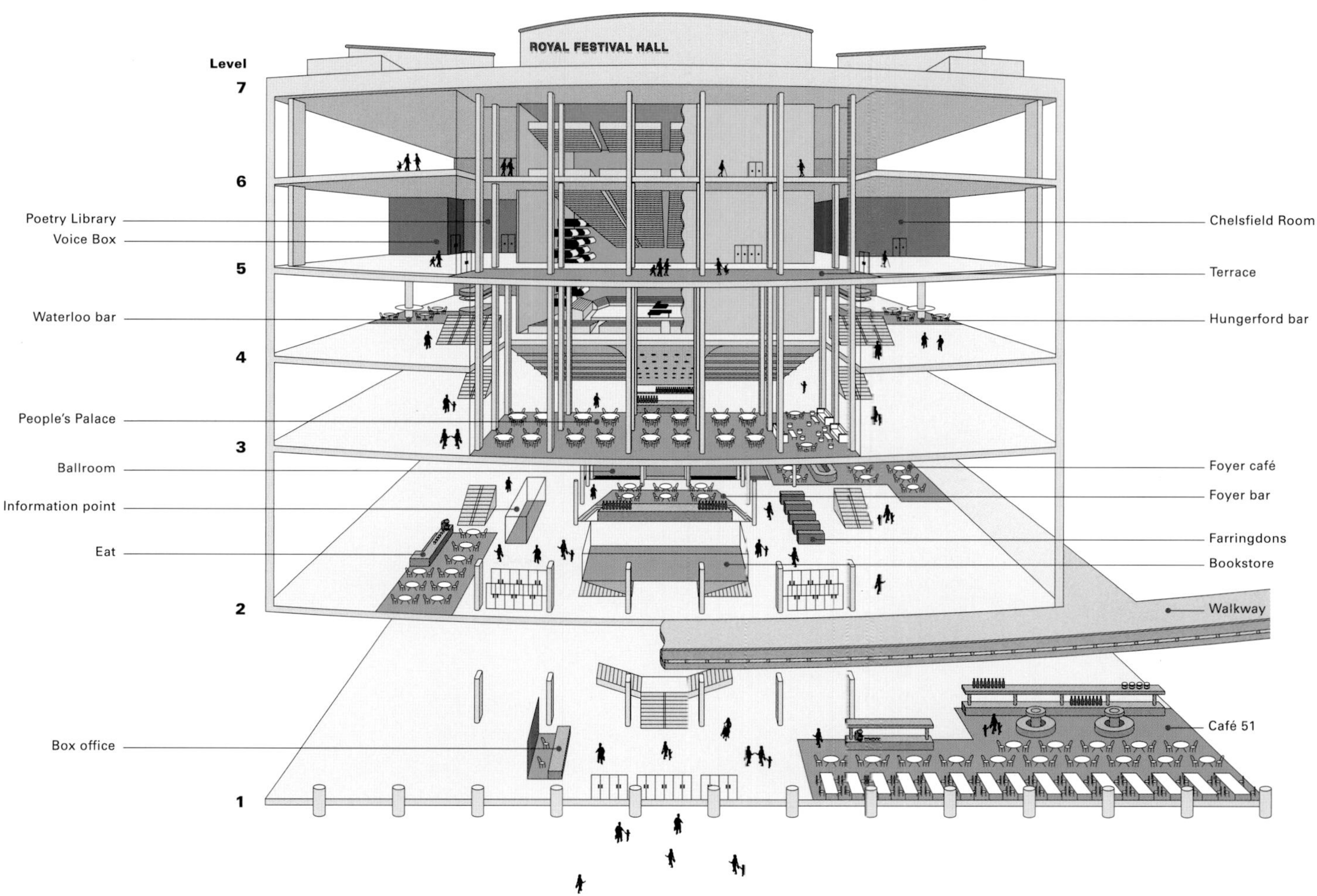

C John Pashe

F South Bank Centre

Tilly Northedge
Sainsbury Distribution Depot

M Digital

B The illustration is to show the features of a new distribution depot built by Sainsburys

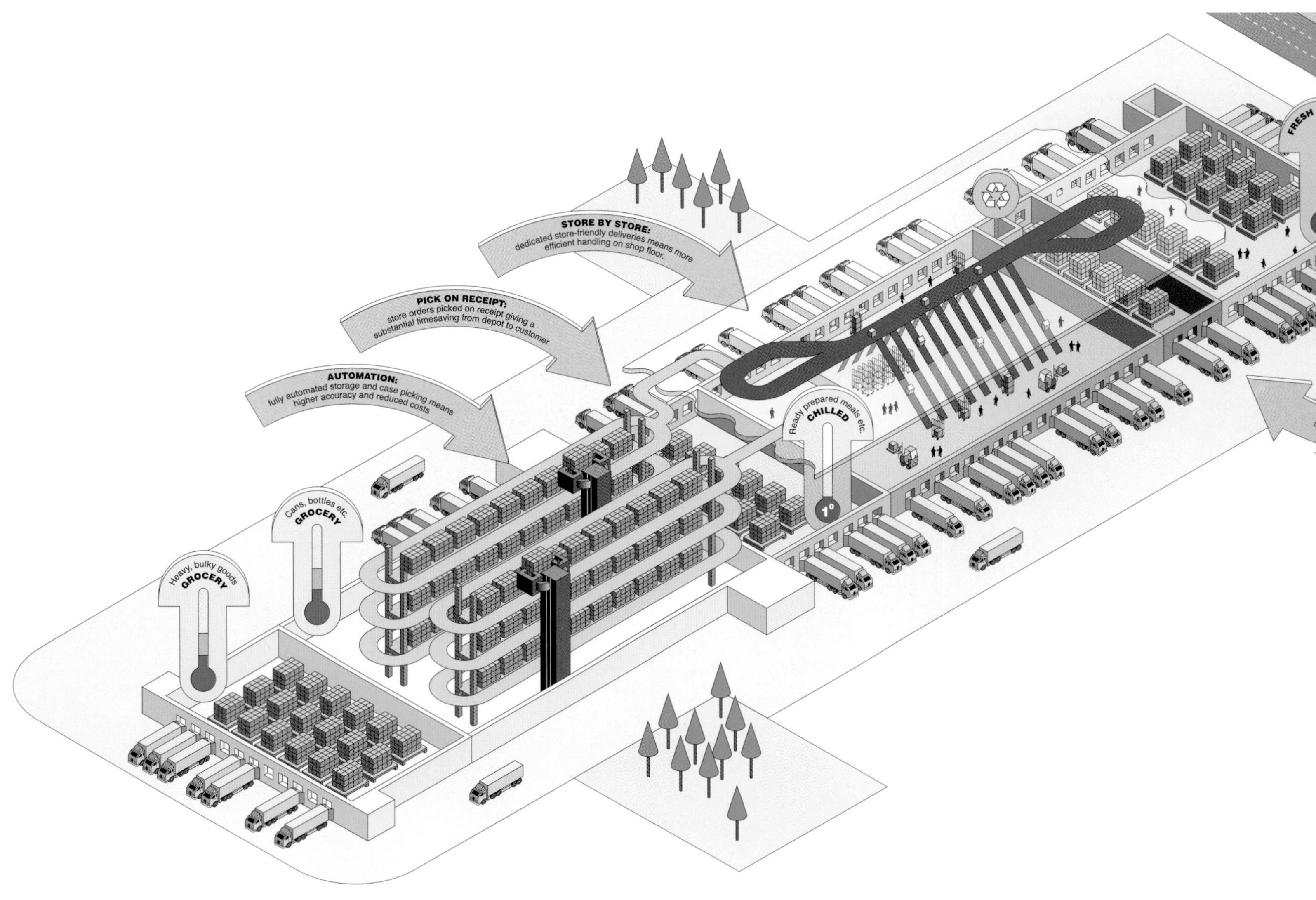

C Louise Cargan

F CGI

Simon Pemberton
(B) Are We Alone in the Universe?
M Mixed media
B Image for 2001 Adobe calendar under the theme 'Are We Alone in the Universe' – if the moon is made of cheese, there is only one answer...

Ashley Potter
Maersk
M Mixed media
B Concept storyboard to depict the transcontinental delivery of services of Maersk (20 second TV commercial)

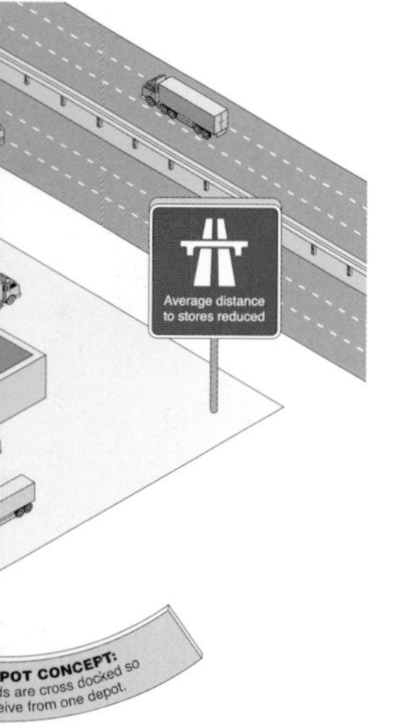

(B)

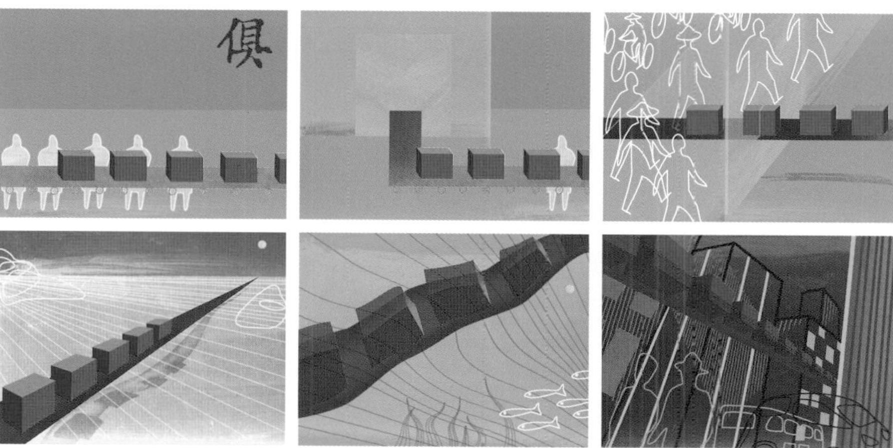

C Paul Hiscock
F Paul Hiscock Design (for Adobe)

C Mario Cavalli
F AKA Pizazz (for Maersk)

Michael Sheehy
New Millennium
M Ink, watercolour
B A New Year's card depicting the passage of time and hope for the future

Lasse Skarbovik
Are We Alone
M Digital
B Illustration for the Adobe System UK Calendar 2001

C Tomas Stavinger
F Gruppe (for DEG)

C Paul Hiscock
F Adobe System UK

Andy Smith
New Directions
M Original art / digital
B Illustration for a catalogue for children's clothes

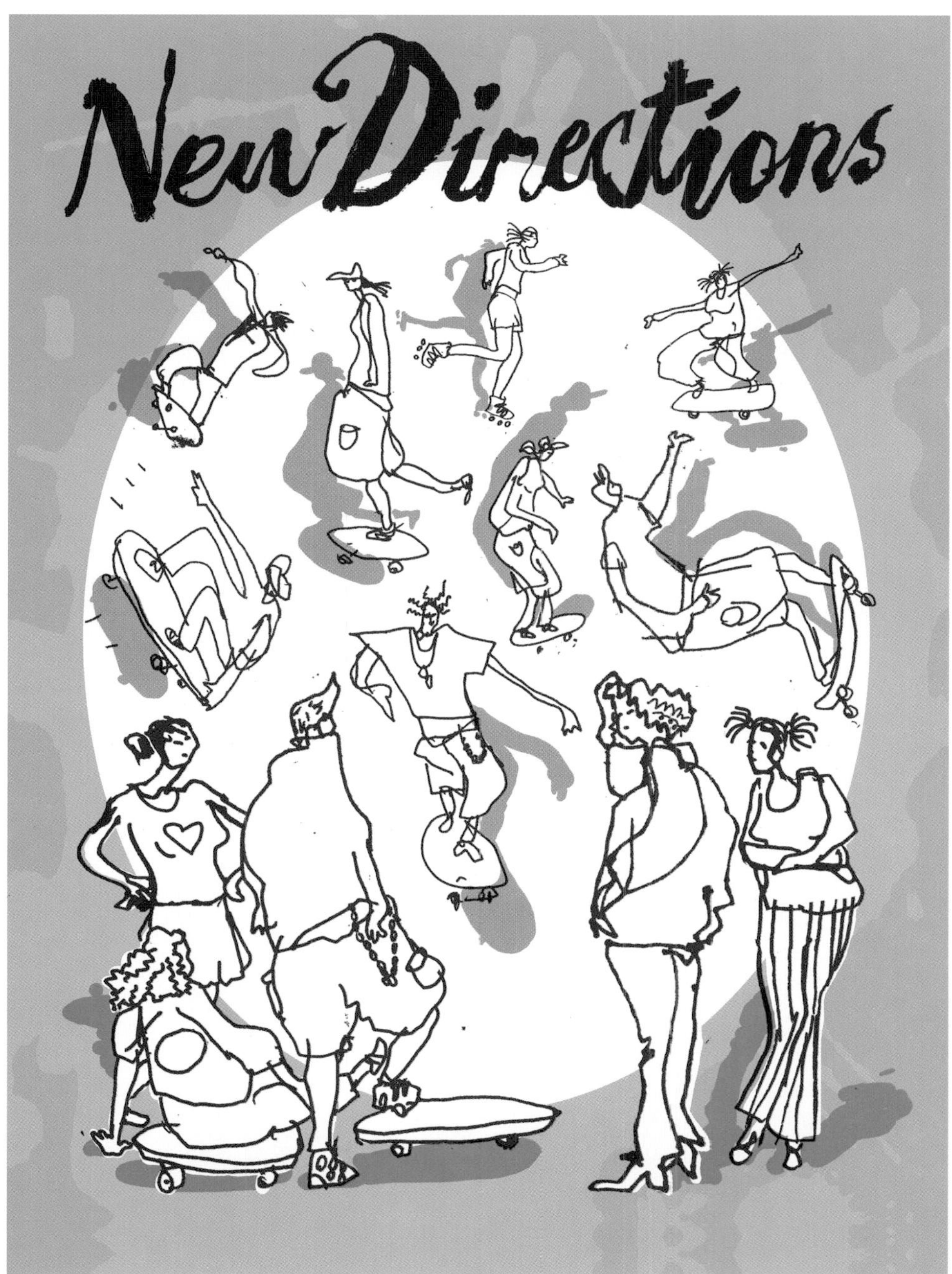

F Explosive

Michelle Thompson
Untitled/Red 9

M Mixed media

B To produce a series of 5 illustrations for a company brochure based on 5 words which International Asset Management felt best described their services

C Steve Edwards

F Pauffley (for International Asset Management)

Untitled/Blue Stripes

M Mixed media

B To produce a series of 5 illustrations for a company brochure based on 5 words which International Asset Management felt best described their services

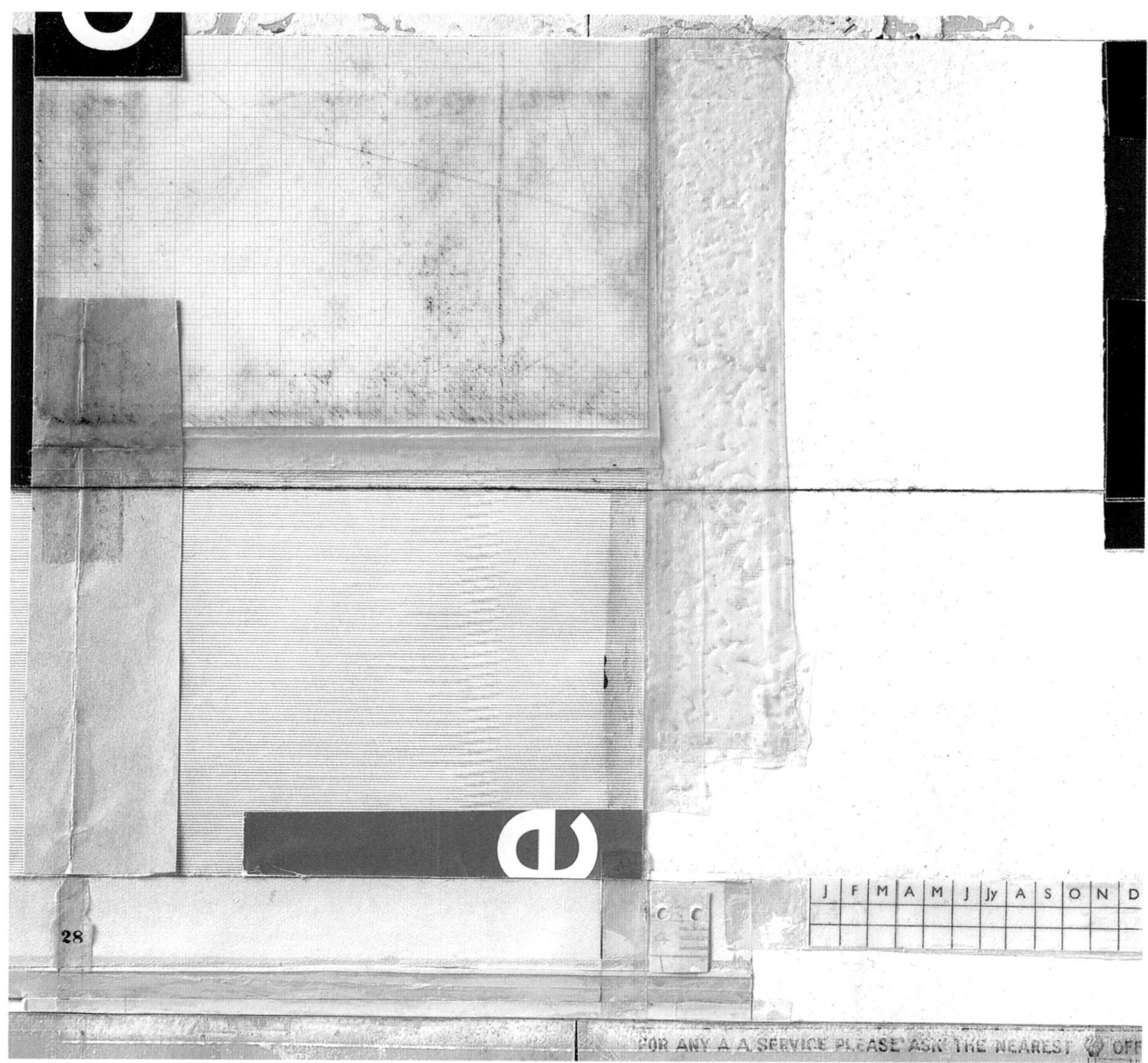

C Steve Edwards

F Pauffley (for International Asset Management)

Bob Venables
Greek Vase

M Alkyd

B The brief required a painting in an antique style to show how a Greek vase may have looked if computers had existed in Ancient Greece

C Keith Perry

F Creative Solutions

Peter Warner
Trill Budgerigar, Cockatiel and Scarlet Macaw
M Watercolour
B Realistic but friendly icons for birdseed packaging. The birds had to be active and behave believably with several objects in a limited area

Own Brand Cat
M Watercolour
B Inquisitive and friendly moggie cat icon for very low budget supermarket cat food packaging. Reproduces small

Cat Chow Delice Cat
M Watercolour
B Cat icon for upmarket cat food packaging. Siamese cat to interact playfully with viewer and pack devices in very restricted space, and be overprintable

C Kerry Willis
F Haines McGregor (for Pedigree Petfoods)

C Jonathan Ragg
F Stocks Taylor Benson

C Alex Barnett
F Ralston Purina Europe SA

Paul Wearing
Leadership
M Digital
B Illustrate the quote 'Destiny is not a matter of chance, but a matter of choice. It is not a thing to be waited for, it is a thing to be achieved', for management training brochure

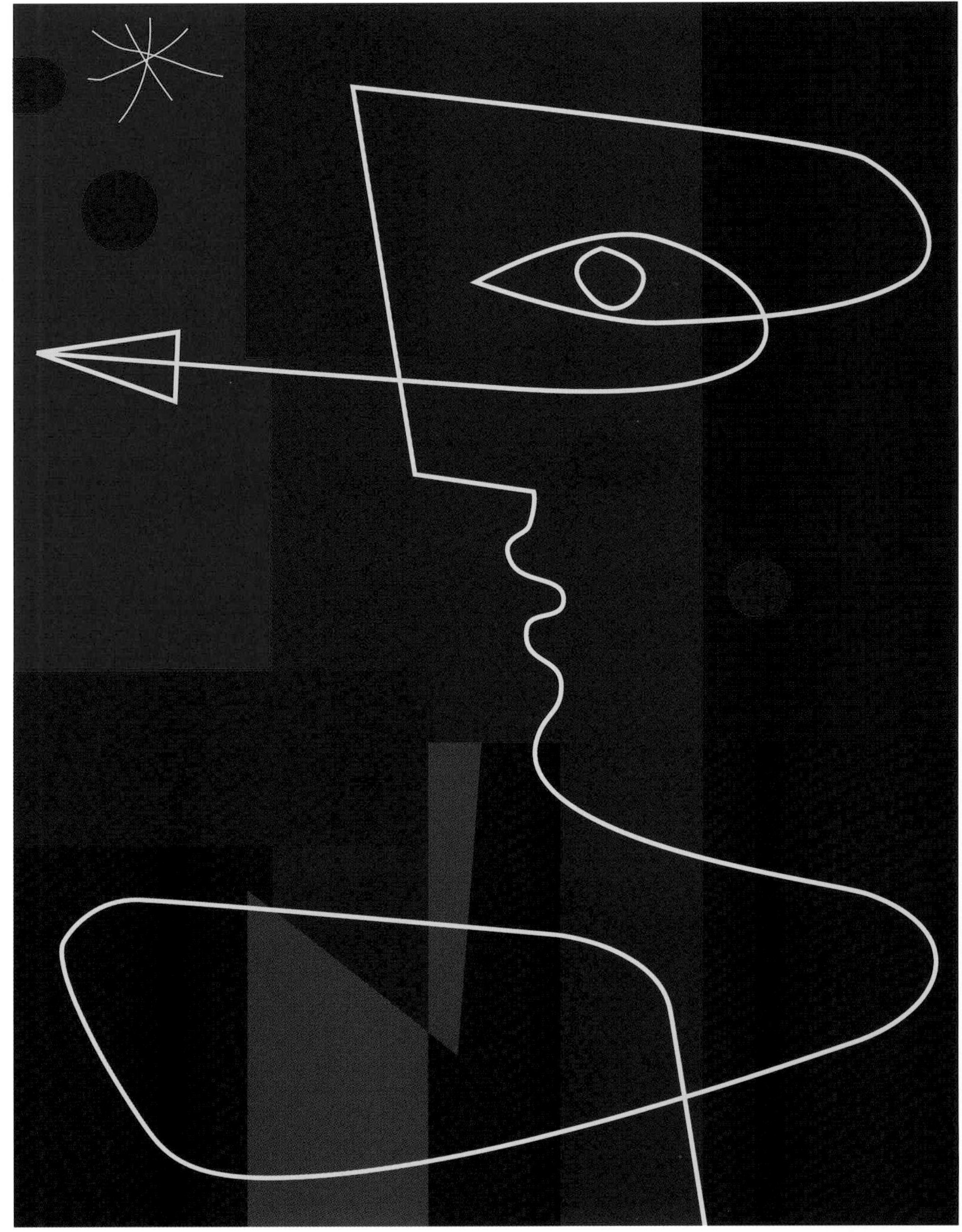

C Mark Self
F MARK SELF DESIGN

Ian Whadcock
E-com Icons

M Digital

B To provide icons for use in a German e-commerce publishers new office building – artwork to be reversed out of white on to glass panels

C Martin Dixon
Freelance Designer

Samantha Wilson

Product Card

Jacuzzi

M Mixed media

B Design promotional postcards to launch a new body to home collection from Nougat

C Flo Brooke

F Nougat Ltd

DEAD LINE

Editorial
Gold award winner

Jason Ford

G Nice Boy, Shame About the Criminal Record

M Mixed media

B These days more and more teenage boys are finding themselves on the wrong side of the law, and not just 'bad' boys from rundown estates

G

C Linda Boyle
Jessica Reiter

F You Magazine

Andy Baker

Thrills and Spills

M Mixed media

B Front cover piece to illustrate a special report on e-commerce

Jump or Be Pushed

M Mixed media

B To illustrate an article on early retirement packages

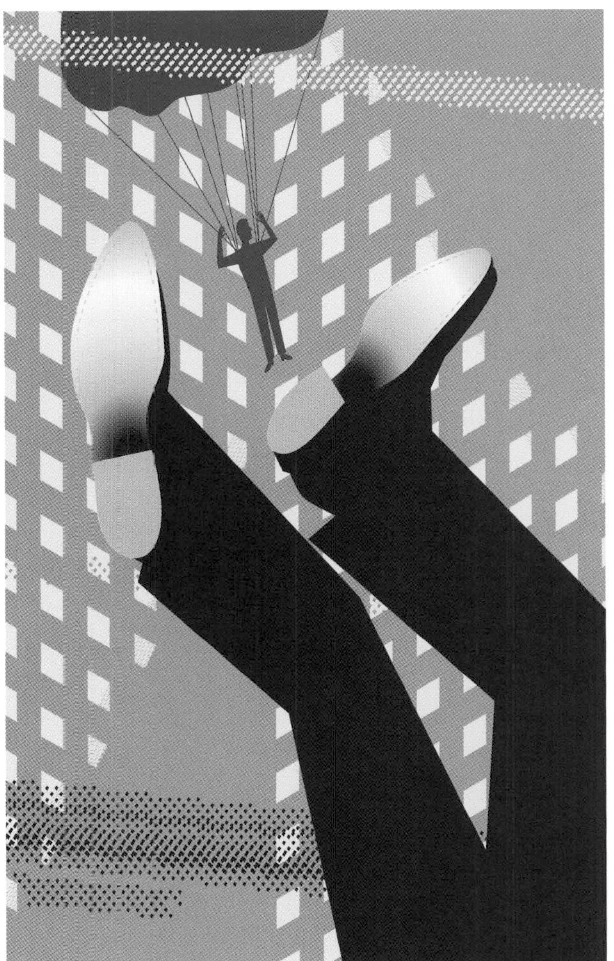

C Suzy Conolly

F The Economist

C Gary Cook

F The Financial Times

Paul Blow

China's Economy

M Acrylic

B To illustrate the problems traditional Chinese business practices have when compared to those in the West

More for Your Mortgage

M Acrylic

B To illustrate how cuts in mortgage rates mean homeowners can get more for their money

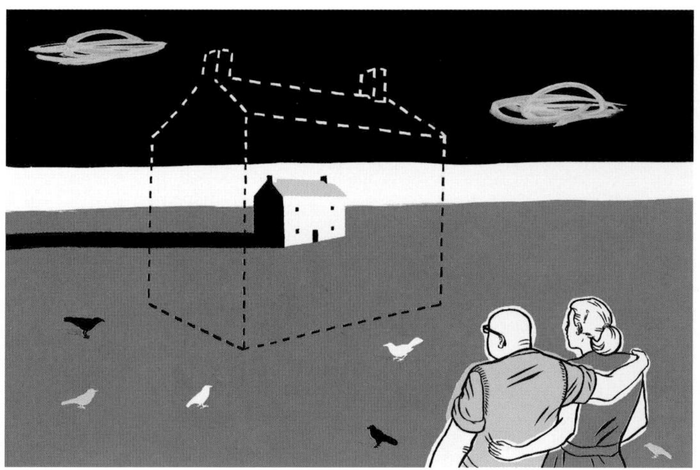

C Anita Wright

F The Economist

C Caroline Williams

F Independent

Stuart Briers
Body Shape
M Digital
B To accompany article about various types of body shape

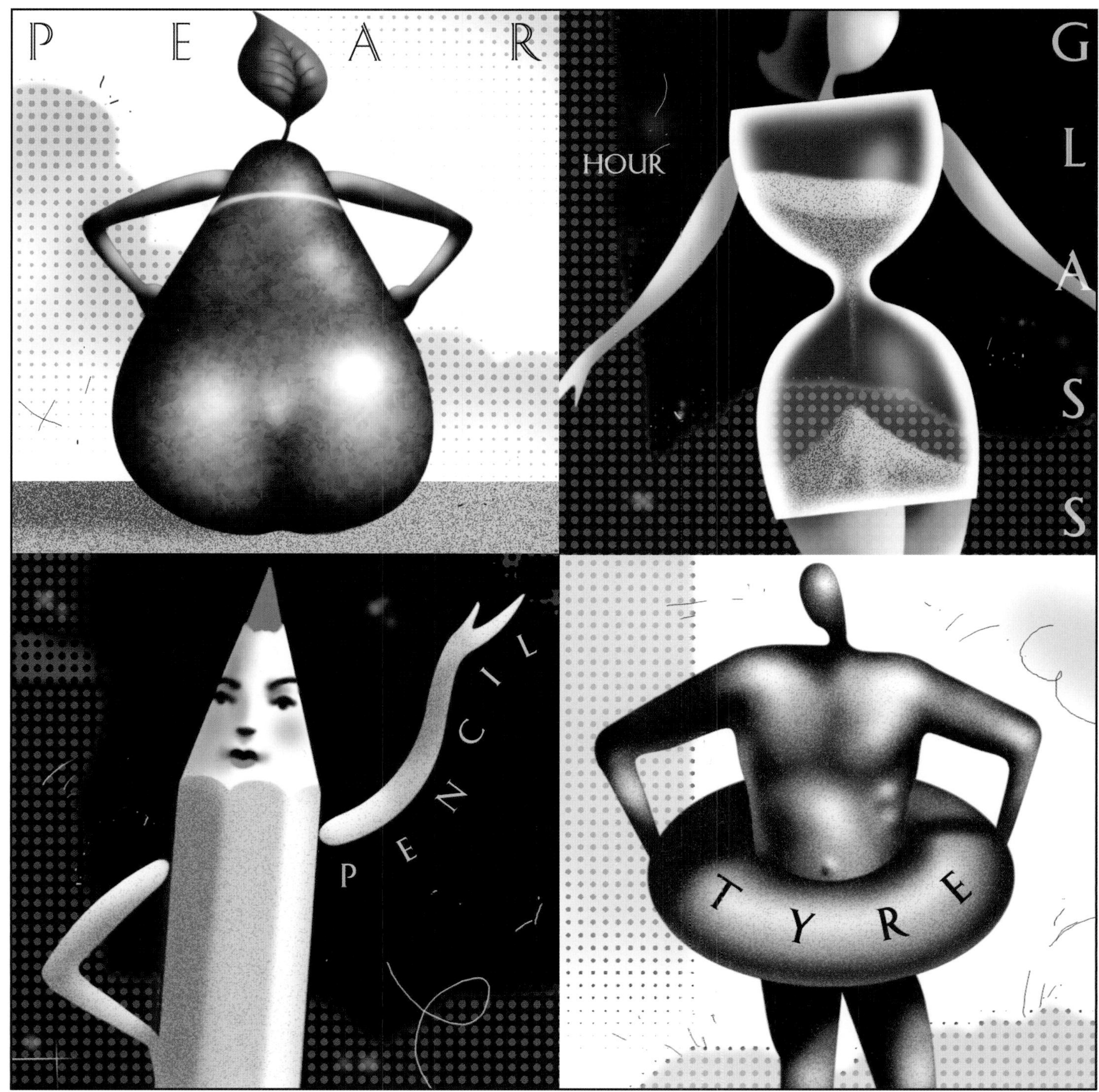

C Natalie Huke
F Express Newspapers

Bill Butcher
Staying Ahead

M Mixed media

B To show the idea of staying ahead of disruptive innovation, for use as a cover illustration

C Brian Saffer

F Financial Times

Graham Carter
Building Men
M Original art / digital
B Based on an extract from a 'Mystery' book

F Sunday Times

Marina Caruso
Astro-Exercise-Libra

M Digital

B To convey the Libran approach to exercise. Basically indulgent. Walking the dog can combine their love of animals, companionship and glamour

Russell Cobb
Forgiveness

M Acrylic

B Forgiveness

C Sarah Snelling

F News International (for Your Destiny Magazine)

C David Golden

F Men's Health Magazine

Russell Cobb
The Bitch Within

M Acrylic

B The bitch within. An article about gossip and loyalty

C Jason Arbuckle

F Emap Elan Network (for Red Magazine)

Brian Cronin
Europe's New Slave Trade

M Ink

B To illustrate article on the illegal trade in immigrants into Europe by modern day 'pirates'

C Martin Colyer

F Reader's Digest

Jonathan Cusick
The Rabbits of Godalming

M Acrylic

B In the 18th century a Godalming housemaid claimed to have given birth to 17 rabbits, a hoax which even duped London's most prominent doctors

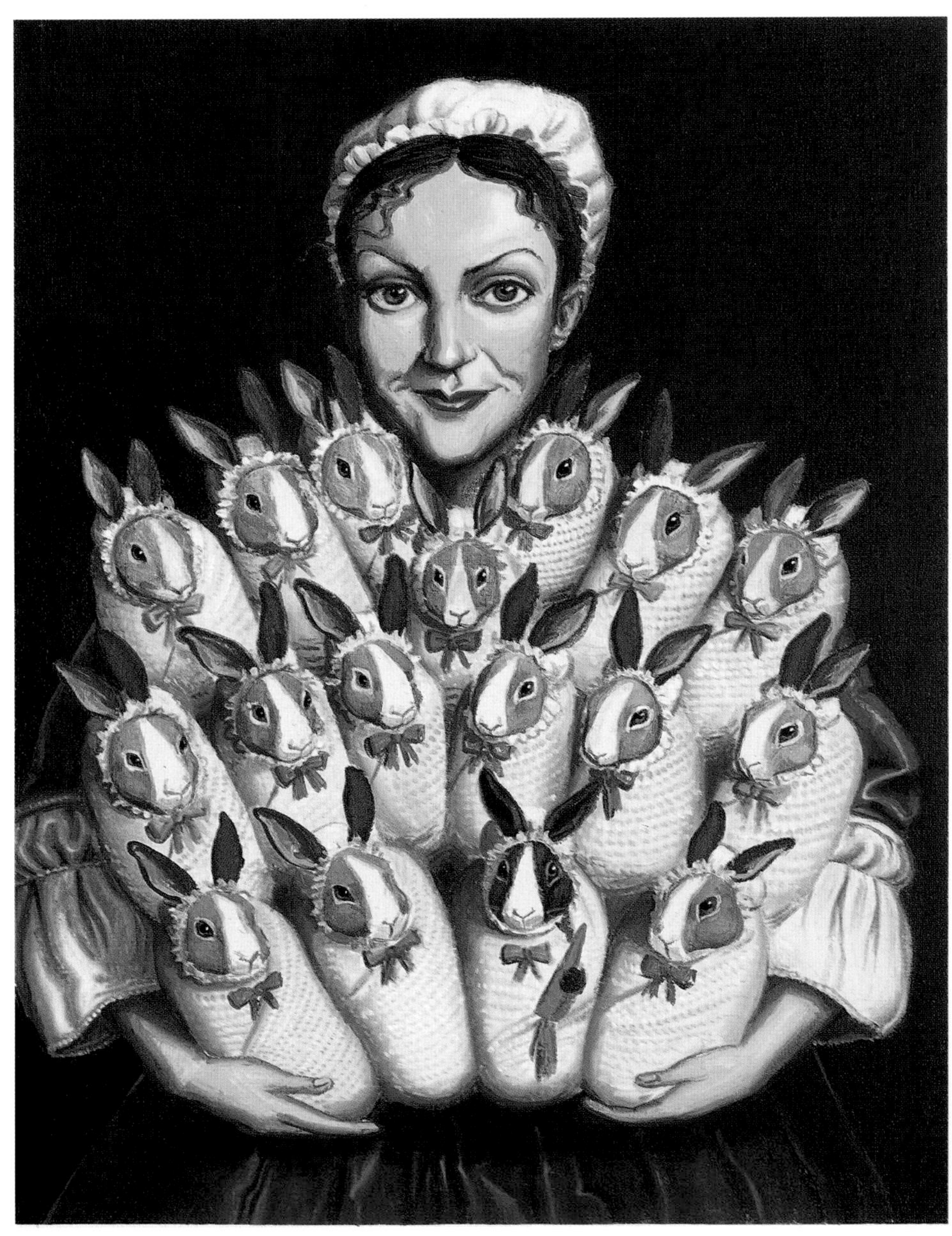

C Caroline Sallis

F BBC Worldwide Ltd (for Radio Times)

Cyrus Deboo

Ⓑ Direct Mail

M Digital

B Cover illustration for Direct Mail supplement

Profitable Customer

M Digital

B Customer relationship management systems implemented by management companies to understand the profile of a profitable customer

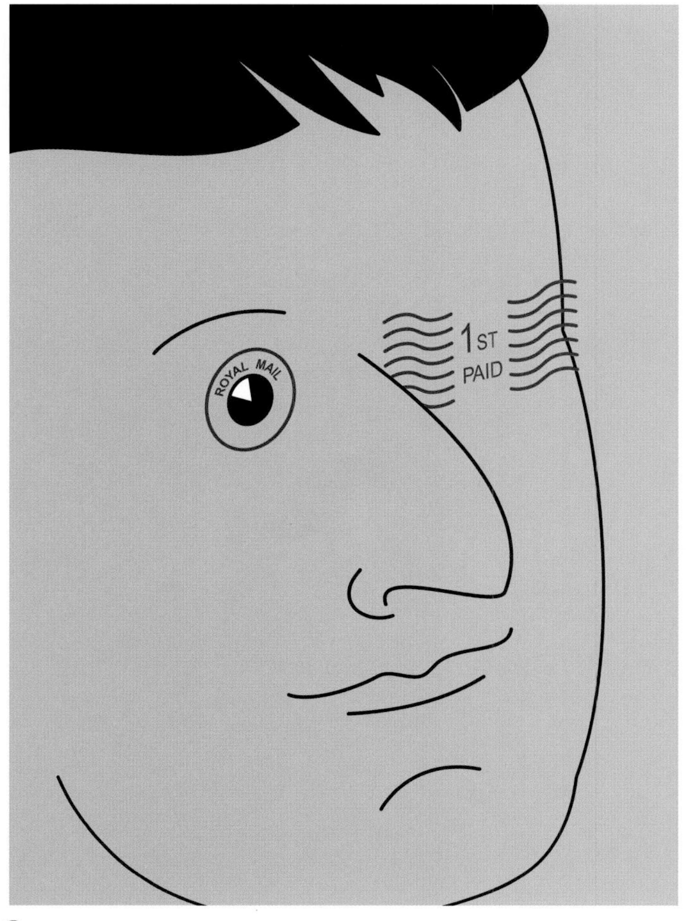

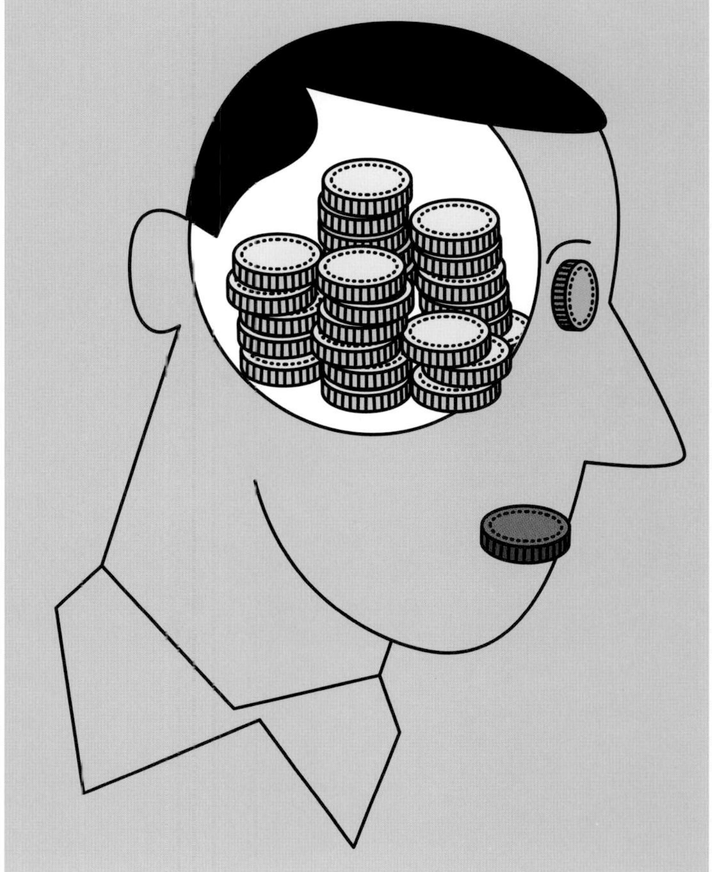

Ⓑ

C Colin McHenry

F Centaur Publishing (for Precision Marketing)

C Colin McHenry

F Centaur Publishing (for Precision Marketing)

Jovan Djordjevic
Blow Me

M Mixed media and digital

B Contemporary expressions and gestures – parodied by the use of an Edwardian steel engraving style

C Ian Robinson

F Stuff Magazine

Red Dot
Digital Corruption

M Mixed media

B Produce an illustration which emphasises the problem of image files 'corrupting' over the internet. A variant of this image is to be used as a front cover

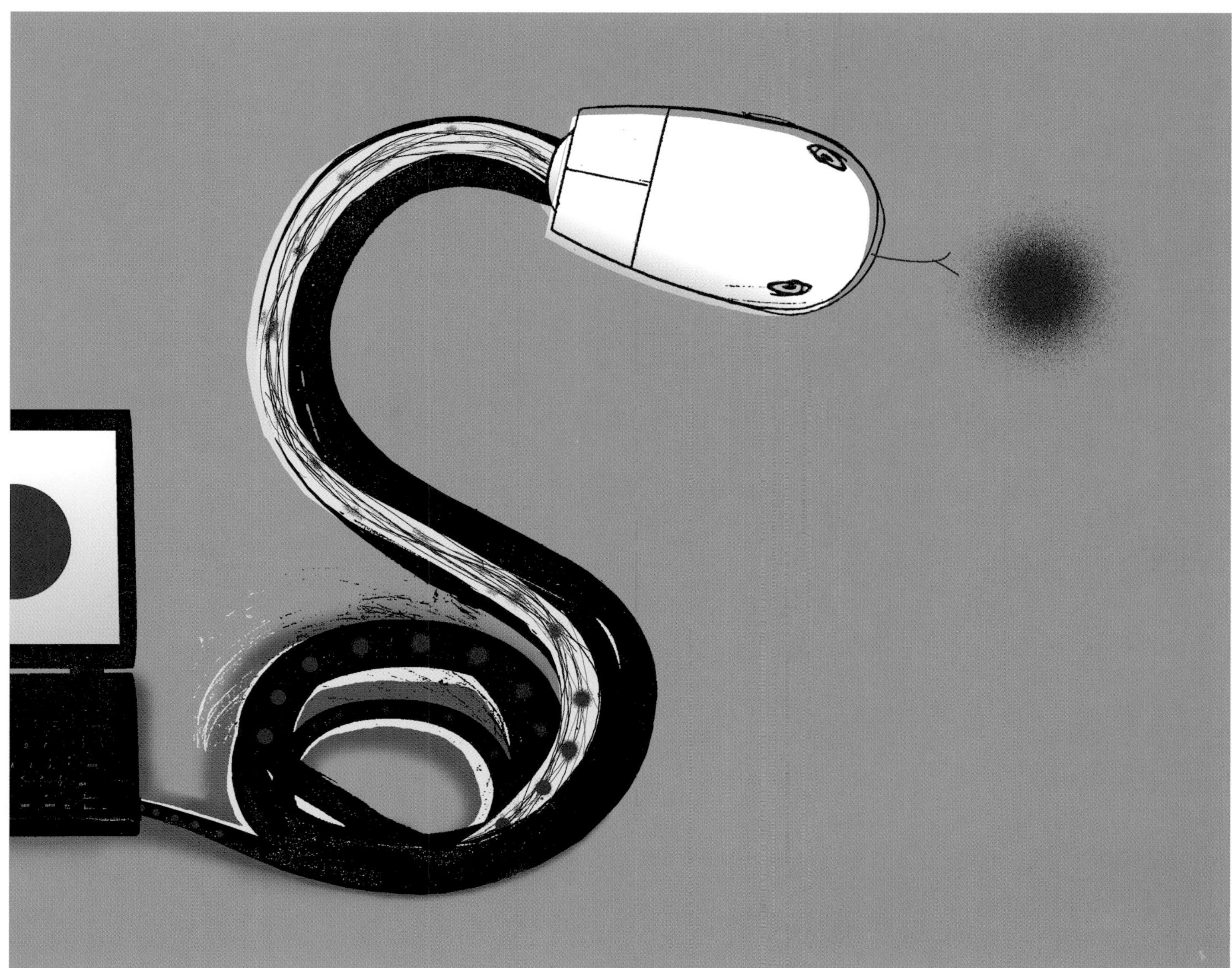

C Richard Krzyzak

F The Builder Group (for Construction Manager)

Simon Farr
Cowboy Builder
M Pen, ink & watercolour
B Article about the disasters of bad builders

C Gordon Beckett
F Sunday Times

Geoff Grandfield
Desire Lines

M Pastel

B Three strangers are travelling their own separate ways late one night. Their paths may cross but they are too engrossed in their own lives to notice

Anne Kristin Hagesaether
The Bridal Bower

M Acrylic

B To illustrate a fiction extract by Rafaella Barker, depicting chaotic and colourful wedding preparations

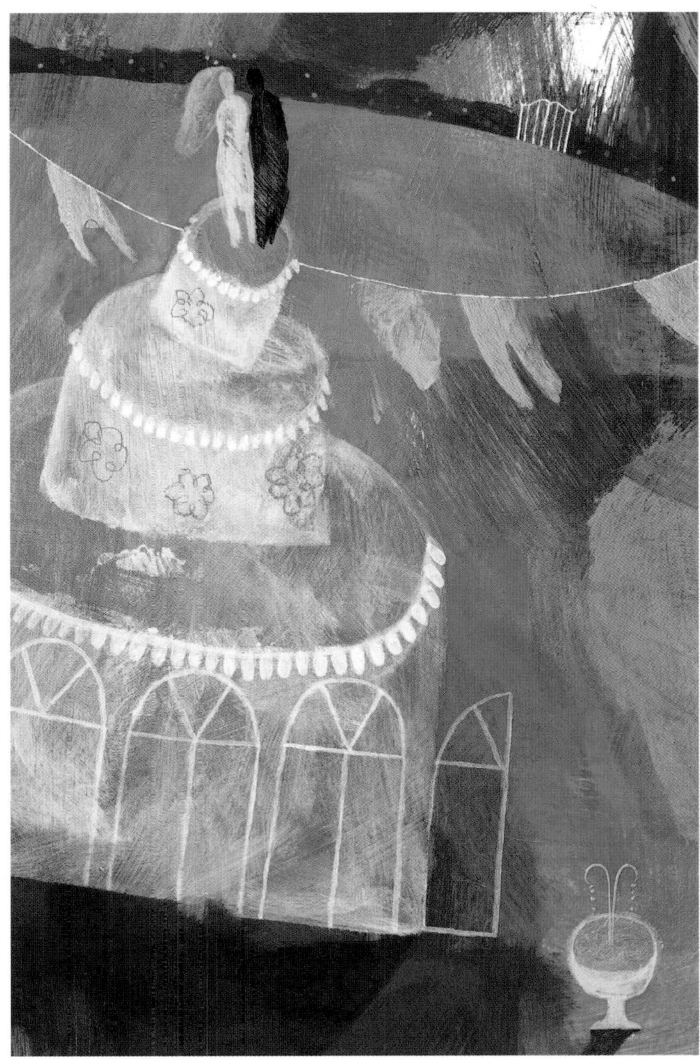

C Tracey Gardiner

F Radio Times

RadioTimes

C Jonathan Christie

F The Independent

Olaf Hajek
Swim wear
Dolce & Gabbana

M Acrylic

B One of full-page illustration for the men's fashion magazine Loaded Fashion – men's accessories

Gucci Surfboard – Men's Accessories

M Acrylic

B One of full-page illustration for the men's fashion magazine Loaded Fashion, – men's accessories 'Gucci Surfboard'

C Konstantin Antonopoulos

F IPC Media, Hatfield House

C Konstantin Antonopoulos

F IPC Media, Hatfield House

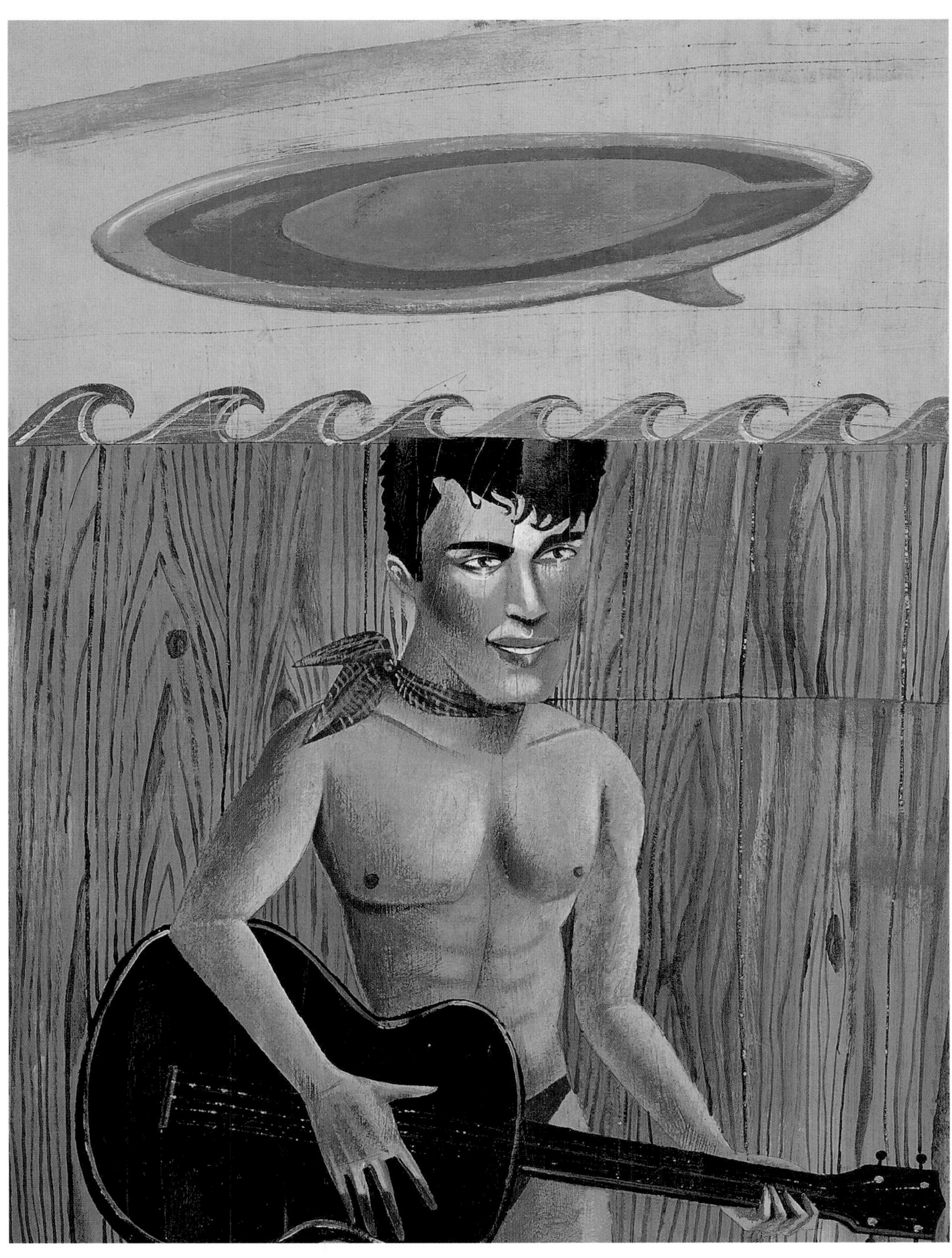

Steve Hambidge

That Sinking Feeling

M Digital

B The public failure of supposedly unsinkable dot.com companies, namely egg.com

Bluetooth

M Digital

B Named after a 15th century Viking, has wireless 'bluetooth' technology lost its bite?

C Wayne Campbell

F Reed Business Information (for IBM Computer Today)

C Paruna Patel

F Reed Business Information (for Micropscope)

Nick Hardcastle
Chapters & Verses
by Michael Field

M Pen, ink, watercolour

B To illustrate a BBC Radio 4 play: the memoirs implied that she might have been having a lesbian affair

C Tracey Gardiner

F BBC Worldwide (for Radio Times)

RadioTimes

Clifford Harper
Losing Words

M Gouache

B To illustrate article on the death of 'regional' language and words

C Martin Colyer

F Reader's Digest

Benoit Jacques

Feng Phooey

M Pen and ink (line and wash)

B Illustrate article on the absurdities of Feng Shui

Top Cat?

M Gouache, pen, ink

B Illustrate quiz article about smartness of cats

C Martin Colyer

F Reader's Digest

C Martin Colyer

F Reader's Digest

Richard Johnson
The Yellow Dress

M Acrylic

B A sympathetic illustration to accompany 'The Yellow Dress', a short story about a man suffering from a mental illness

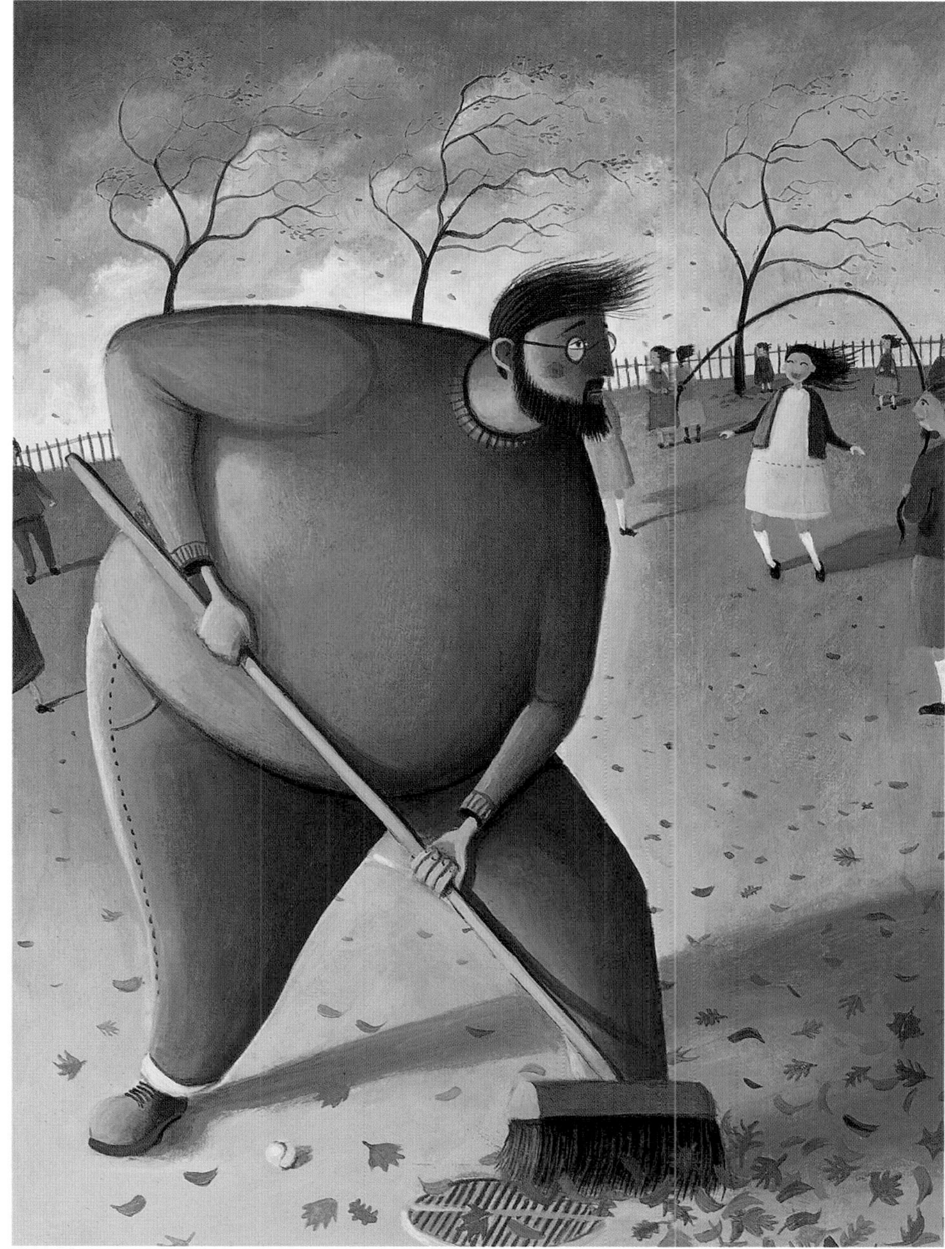

C Ajoa Yeboah-Afari

F Commonwealth Secretariat

Matthew Johnson

Homework

M Mixed media

B To describe the situation of the modern homeworker

Nightmare Restaurant

M Mixed media

B Reader survey on bad restaurants, featuring livestock, organ music and a sinister maitre d'

F John Brown Publishing

C Wayne Ford

F Observer Newspaper

Satoshi Kambayashi

Green Investment

M Line & wash

B Investments which take the environment into account are doing better than ever

Work Equipment Failure

M Line & wash

B Article about strict liability for work equipment, which includes a case of a postman injured through a bicycle failure

Hunt for Liquidity

M Digital

B The race is on for the stock exchanges of Europe, for the survival of the biggest – competition is tough as liquidity is not aplenty

C Selwyn Cox

F BBC WorldWide (for BBC Wildlife)

C Dana Mansfield

F Butterworths (for New Law Journal)

C Penny Garrett Dominic Ziegler

F The Economist

Chris Kasch
Art For Hire

M Acrylic

B Editorial discussing artwork for hire (Hockney, etc) in the home. The feel of the room needed to be representative of Elle magazine

Sean Lee
Ground Force's Tommy Walsh – caricature

M Gouache

B Caricature for regular 'Questionnaire' piece – Ground Force's Tommy Walsh is placed in a gardening related scenario

C Jo Sams

F Elle Magazine

C Paul Smith

F Radio Times

RadioTimes

Henning Löhlein
Evolution of Portable Computers

M Acrylic

B To depict the development of mobile computing

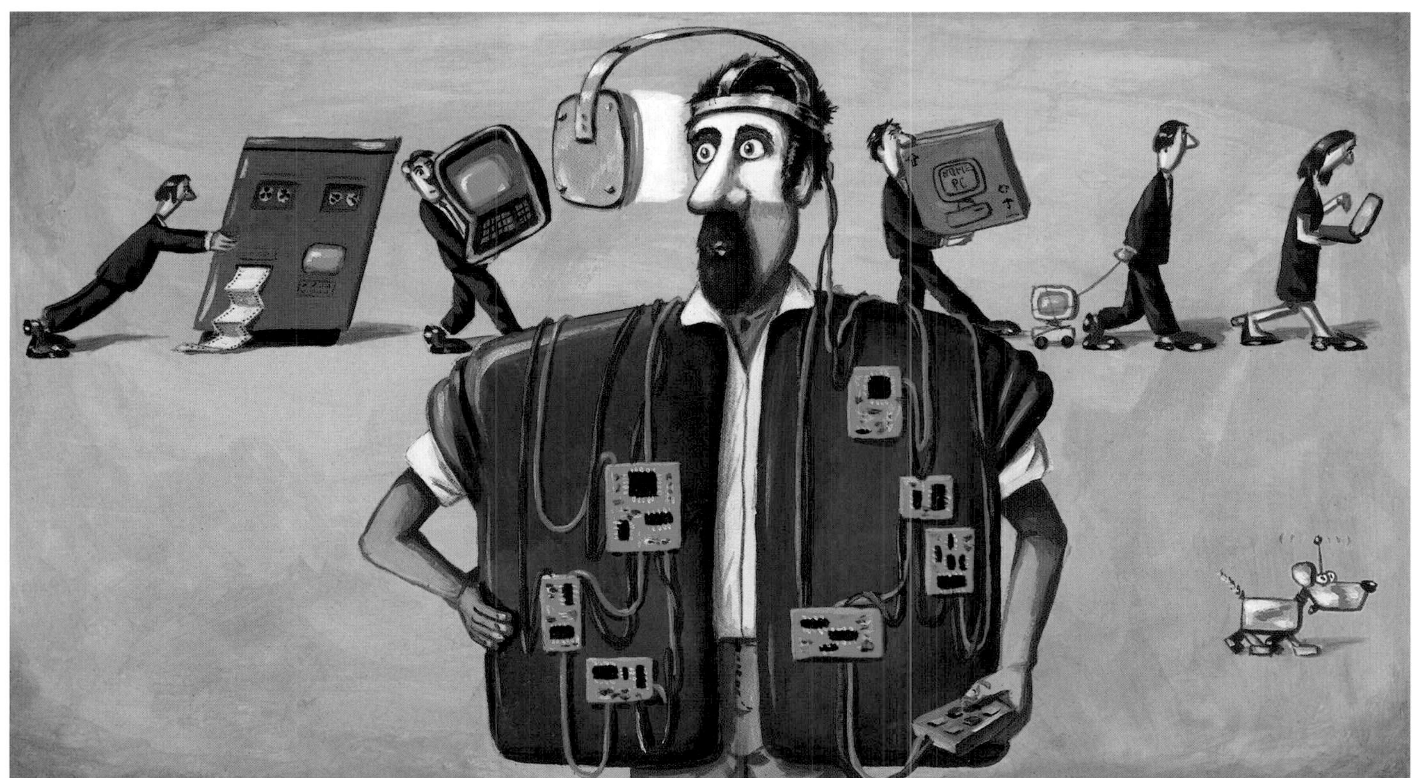

F The Guardian

James Marsh

Europe's Stolen Children

M Acrylic, collage

B To illustrate article on 'tug of love' children in Europe

Green with Envy

M Acrylic on canvas

B Open brief to illustrate feature article about repayment of student loan

The Tomorrow Trap

M Acrylic on canvas

B Open brief to illustrate feature article about how to avoid the pitfalls of planning for retirement

C Martin Colyer

F Reader's Digest

C Dane Wilson

F Times Newspapers (for TES)

C Victoria Nightingale

F Reader's Digest

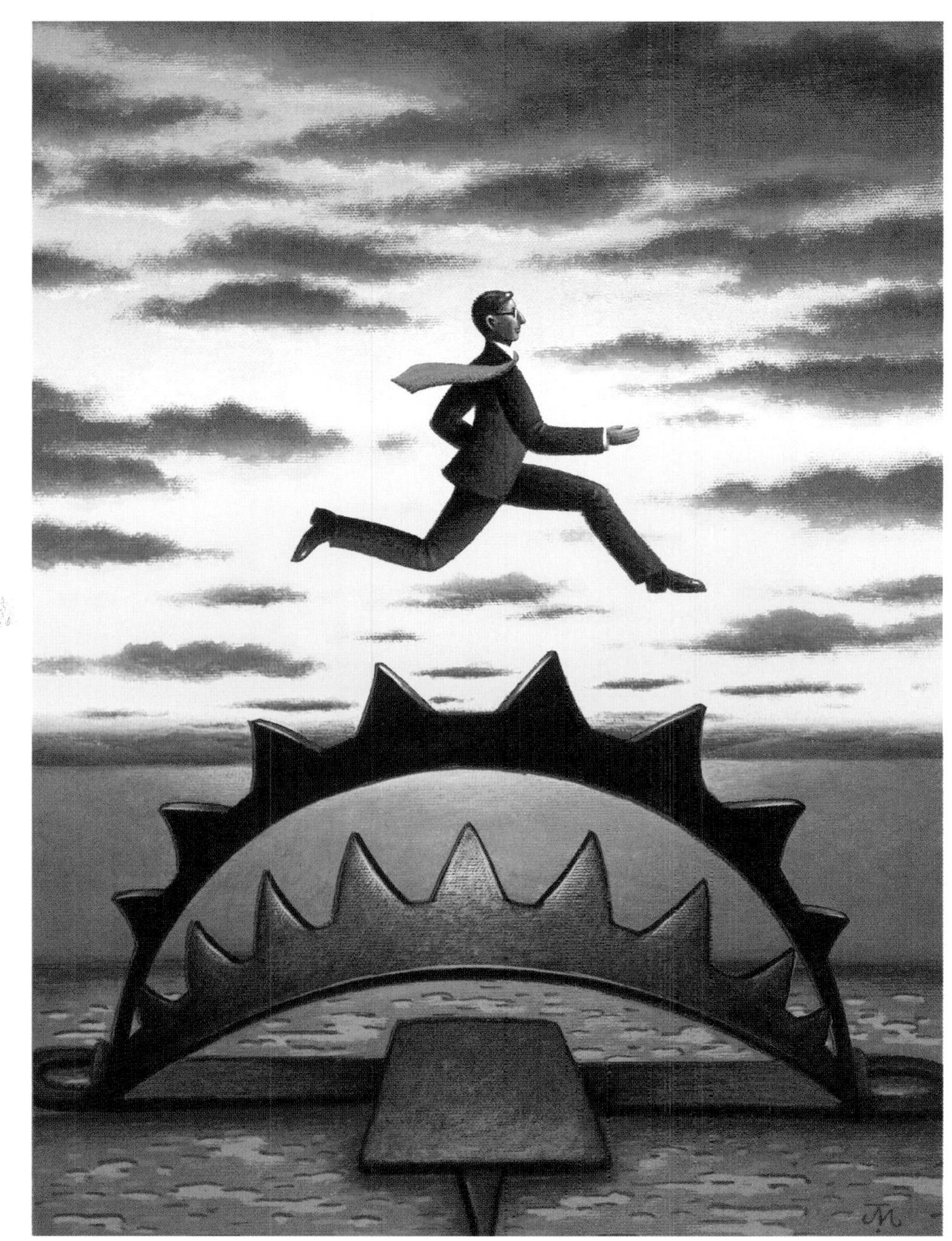

Shane Mc Gowan

Super Accountant

M Digital

B To show that accountants are fabulous and you really need one because they bust through all that boring book work

C Andrew Butterworth

F Reader's Digest (for Moneywise)

Caged Bird

M Digital

B In a sensitive way illustrate Concorde's plight, the week after the crash

C Kate Ward

F Time/Life (for Time Magazine)

Dating Hell

M Digital

B To illustrate an article about the many types of dreadful date, in this case the self obsessed and the piggy eater

Sex-pots and Sexspots

M Digital

B To illustrate the review of a book that talks about the sexual exploits of famous queers on their worldly travels in the last century

C Carol Anderson

F The Express

C Glen Platts

F Gay Times

Belle Mellor

Teddy Rack

M Pen and ink (line and wash)

B Illustration of a toy tester for a column about people with unusual jobs

Snow Business

M Pen and ink (line and wash)

B Illustration of a manufacturer of artificial snow

Spaghetti

M Pen and ink (line and wash)

B Illustration of a food stylist

From Maggot to Fly

M Pen and ink (line and wash)

B Illustration of a man who studies maggots and their development

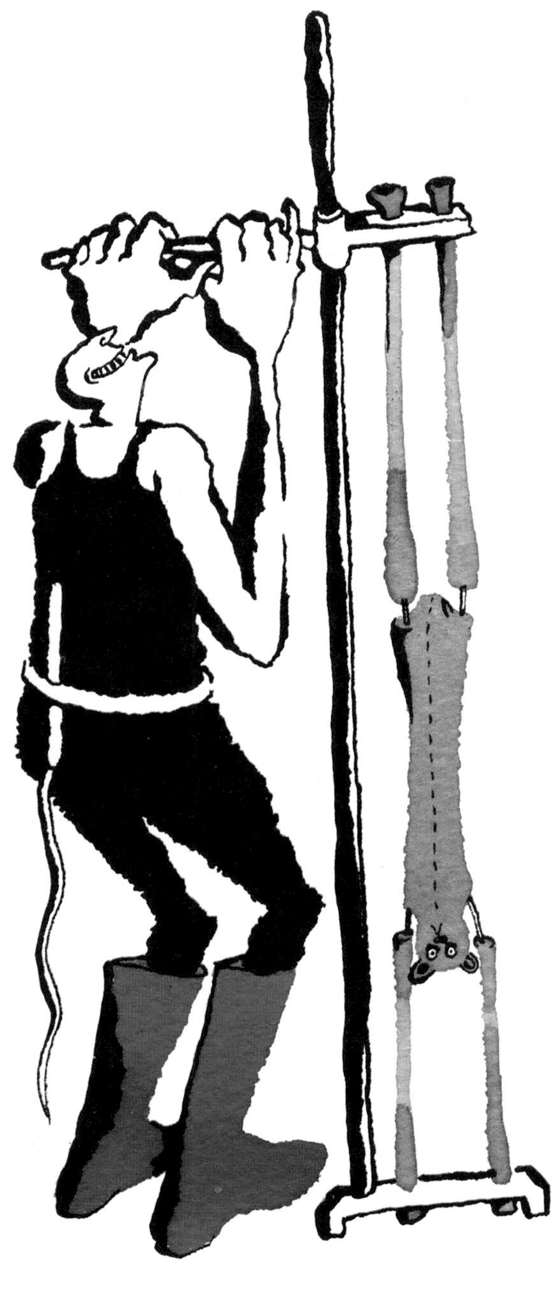

C Graham Ball
F Times Magazine

C Graham Ball
F Times Magazine

C Graham Ball
F Times Magazine

C Graham Ball
F Times Magazine

José Luis Merino

When Mothers Lose That Loving Feeling

M Mixed media

B These days women are expected to fall head over heels with their offspring. But what if all you feel is indifference?

When Your Child Plays Gooseberry

M Mixed media

B Children always come first. Or do they? Some parents are so devoted to each other, they leave their offspring on the sidelines

C Linda Boyle

F You Magazine

C Linda Boyle

F You Magazine

Kate Miller
The Truth About Love and Marriage

M Digital

B Article about the rising divorce rates amongst newly-weds, due to a lack of freedom

C Ben Brannan

F Guardian Magazine

Gunnlaug Moen Hembery
About Having it in the Back of the Head

M Mixed media

B Editorial for leading Norwegian newspaper. Text written by Selma Lønning Aarø. About the trauma of going to the hairdressers, and being measured in all directions by a stranger

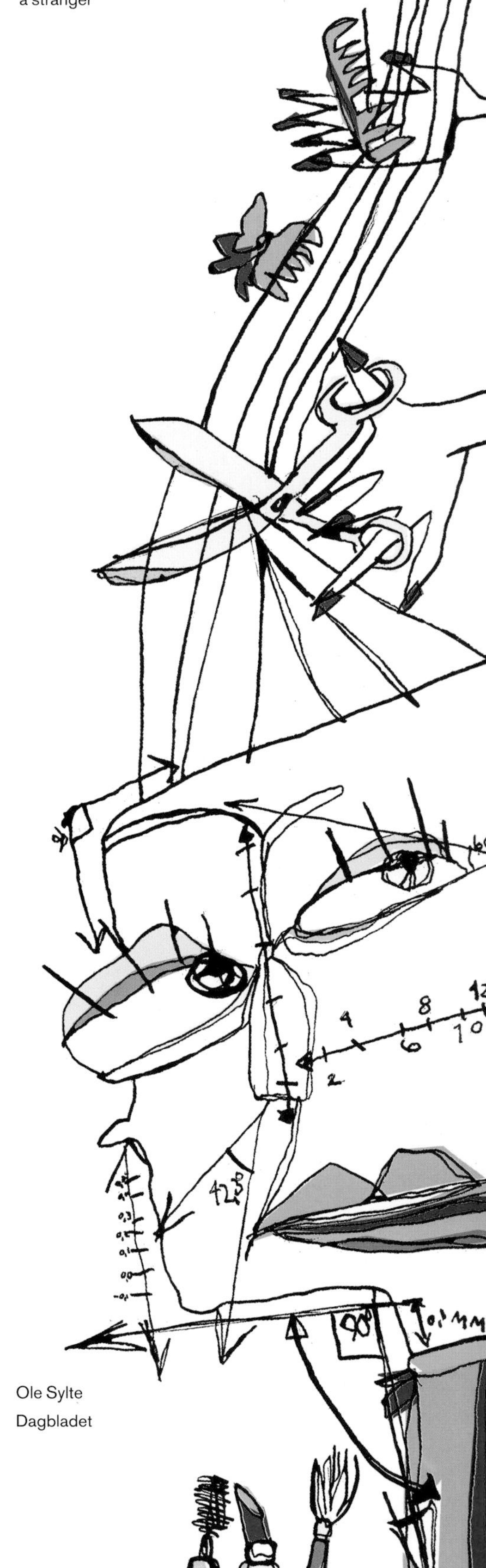

C Ole Sylte

F Dagbladet

Ian Murray

Road Kill

M Digital, pen & ink

B Article on 'strange laws' – illustrate Virginian State Law in which the driver must collect and eat animals killed after being struck by their vehicle

C Jan Warren

F John Brown Publishing (for WHS Total Guides – Know Your Rights)

Eco-Hotel

M Digital, pen & ink

B Represent how hotel businesses are attempting to integrate their buildings into the landscape. Encouraging wildlife and incorporating resource / energy saving measures at the same time

C Keely Mitchell

F Reed Business Information (for Caterer & Hotel Keeper Magazine)

Smart Card

M Digital, pen & ink

B To illustrate the range of goods and services that a hotel sponsored smartcard would hold information about and help pay for, during someone's stay

C Keely Mitchell

F Future Publishing (for Caterer & Hotel Keeper Magazine)

I Love Ewe

M Digital, pen & ink

B Article on 'strange laws' – in Montana it is illegal for a man to carry a sheep in the cab of his truck without a chaperone

C Jan Warren

F John Brown Publishing (for WHS Total Guides – Know Your Rights)

Chuck's
TRUCKS

Arnie Nisbet
Elvis Impersonator
M Digital
B Cover illustration for an article about contemporary Elvis impersonators

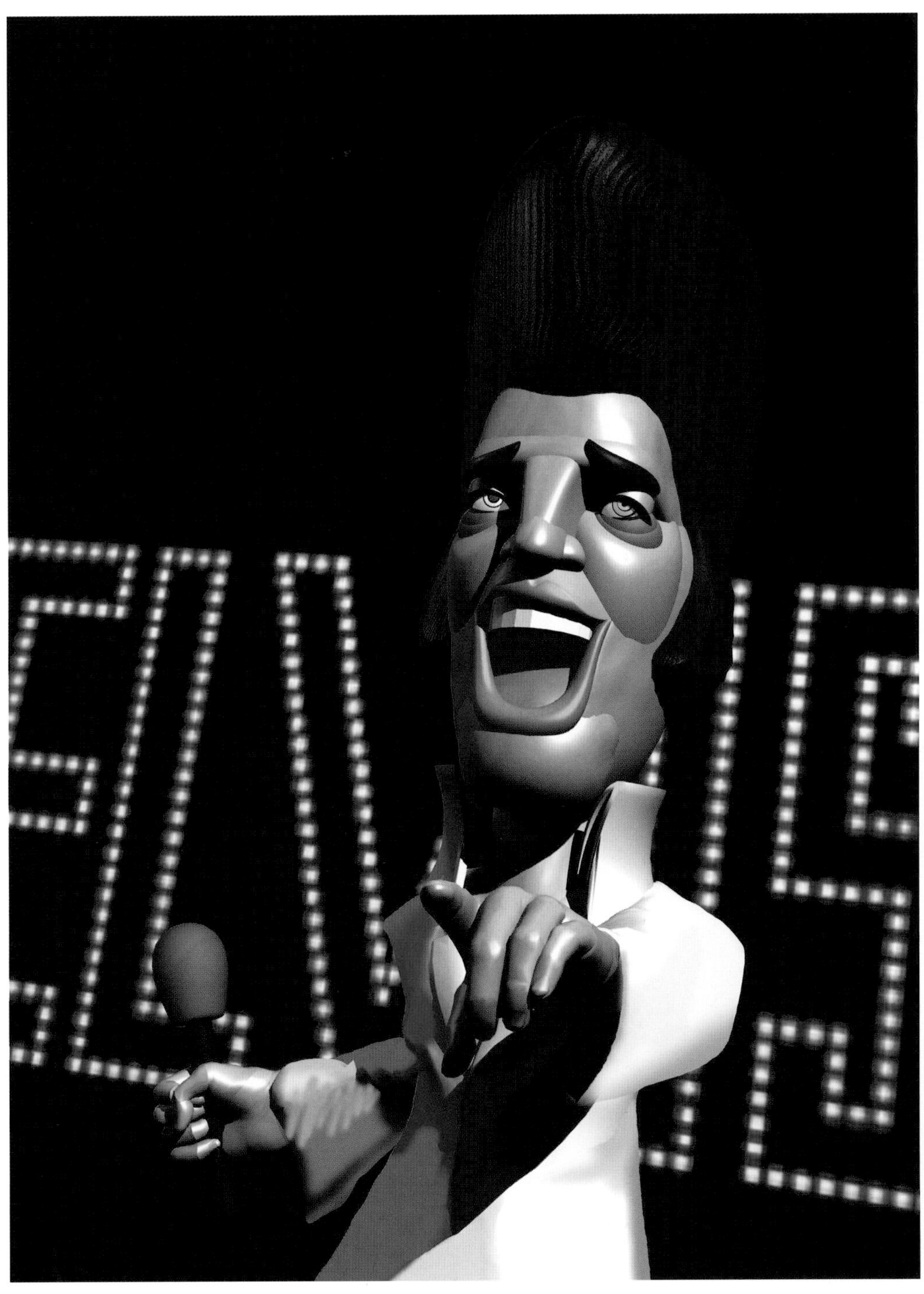

C Rob Cannon
F Big Issue Scotland

Kevin O'Keefe

Head/Clouds

M Ink, photoshop

B Small businesses may chase debts and charge interest on late payments. Big businesses have avoided their attentions by appearing small themselves, soon to change however

Mouse/Elephant

M Ink, photoshop

B Article on legal conflict in Building magazine. The triumphant elephant (client) believes he is safe from attack by the mouse

Room/Room

M Ink, photoshop

B In the legal dispute Karl Vs. Sweeney, the adjudicator was generally inaccessible. Listening only to her own counsel, her discussion was consequently somewhat colourless

Tightrope

M Ink, photoshop

B To provide a drawing of a suited gent walking, within a cityscape, a financial tightrope, balancing on the one hand cash, on the other, ISAs

C Jonathan Deayton
F Builder Group

C Jonathan Deayton
F Builder Group

C Jonathan Deayton
F Builder Group

F Charterhouse Communications

Martin O'Neill
Forgery!
M Collage
B To illustrate with relevant images a story about forgery

Nigel Owen
S State of the Menu
M Digital
B To illustrate the changing nature of menus, reflecting the wider choice throughout the day that is now available to the customer

S

C Martin Colyer
F Reader's Digest

C Beth Meyers
F Restaurant Biz Magazine (US)

Paquebot
Mixed Messages

M Digital

B Illustrate an article about Meltzer commission report which has internal contradictions

C Susan Buchanan

F Buchanan-Davey (for Worldlink)

Garry Parsons
Sardine Air

M Acrylic

B Why Henry Mintzberg hates flying

C Elizabeth Jordan

F Reuters

Ali Pellatt
Edinburgh Festival

M Mixed media, photoshop

B To illustrate the energy, creativity and madness of the Edinburgh Festival

C Mark Leeds

F The Guardian

Simon Pemberton

Super Surfer

M Mixed media

B Full page illustration comparing 'next generation' mobiles that really can surf to WAP phones that are useless at it

Don't Be Afraid

M Mixed media

B To illustrate people's fear of on-line banking and the idea that no-one wants to be the first to get their fingers bitten

Keeping in Touch

M Mixed media

B To illustrate the idea of new mobile phone technology that means you can stay in touch no matter where you are

C Darren Endicott

F Future Publishing (for Business 2.0)

C Gavin Brammall

F Guardian / Observer

C Gavin Brammall

F Guardian / Observer

Ingram Pinn
International Justice

M Pen and ink

B To illustrate an article about Milosevic and international justice

C Brana Radovic

F Financial Times

Ian Pollock
Is Anyone Listening?

M Watercolour, ink, gouache

B Viewers are unable to tell programme-makers to see sense when they go wrong

C Tracey Gardiner

F Radio Times, (BBC Worldwide)

Shonagh Rae
How A Blood Clot Changed My Life

M Mixed media

B Recent news stories about long haul air travel have highlighted the dangers of deep vein thrombosis (DVT), but it's not just travellers at risk

C Linda Boyle

F You Magazine

Nik Ramage
The Festive Family Feud

M Pen, rubberstamp

B It's supposed to be the season of goodwill, so why is Christmas often the catalyst for a major family bust-up?

C Suzanne Davies

F You Magazine

Darren Raven
Upwardly Mobile
M Digital
B To illustrate article on mobile phone use in Finland

C Martin Colyer
F Reader's Digest

Maria Raymondsdotter

Mobile Girl
M Mixed media
B To illustrate an article about Japan and the Japanese culture
C Wayne Ford
F The Observer

His Ex
M Mixed media
B To illustrate a man dining out with his wife and the ex
C Carolyn Roberts
F Independent

The Workgroup
M Mixed media
B To illustrate people with ethnic diversity within a group of people who are in a workgroup
C Allinda Hardwick
F The Industry Standard

Chris Robson

What Lies Beneath

M Digital

B Double page spread about the unseen players who keep the internet running smoothly

City Hospital

M Digital

B Guardian Society supplement cover: specialised teams sent into run down inner city areas to reinvigorate them

Ram Man

M Digital

B The Apple Mac Circus Sideshow

Away from the glare of publicity are the unsung heroes of the Net. You might have a great site, or even a great business, but without them you'd be lost. Bill Thompson introduces the people who get the internet to work every day– the backroom players

What lies beneath

So it's finally happened: your dotcom startup idea for selling reconditioned Spectrum computers online was a big hit at First Tuesday and now you've got £5 million to burn through before the venture capitalists move in and reduce your beautiful dream to another dull retail outlet in the information supermall.

If you're going to turn your dodgy business plan into a viable dotcom (or even a non-viable dotcom, since these people don't care wether you make money as long as you pay for their services up front) you'll need some help. Lots of help.

Fortunately there are thousands of companies, small and large, out there to provide everything you could possibly need to build and maintain an internet presence. Many of them work in

If you're going to turn your dodgy business plan into a viable dotcom (or even a non-viable dotcom, since these people don't care wether you make money as long as you pay for their services up front) you'll need some help. Lots of help.

Fortunately there are thousands of companies, small and large, out there to provide everything you could possibly need to build and maintain an internet presence. Many of them work in

What is a backroom player?

selling reconditioned Spectrum computers online was a big hit at First Tuesday and now you've got £5 million to\ your beautiful dream to another dull retail outlet in the information supermall.

nally happened: your dotcom startup idea for selling reconditioned Spectrum computers onli big hit at First Tuesday and now you've got £5 your beautiful dream to another dull retail information supermall.

If you're going to turn your dodgy business dotcom (or even a non-viable dotcom, sincet care wether you make money as long services up front) you'll need some help.

Your dotcom startup idea for selling reconditioned Spectrum computers online was a big hit at First Tuesday and now you've got £5 million to burn through before the venture capitalists move in and reduce your beautiful dream to another dull retail outlet in the information supermall.

If you're going to turn your dodgy business plan into a viable dotcom (or even a non-viable dotcom, since these people don't care wether you make money as long as you pay for their services up front) you'll need some help. Lots of help.

Fortunately there are thousands of companies, small and large, out there to provide everything you could possibly need to build and maintain an internet presence. Many of them work in

Who can help?

If you're going to turn your dodgy business plan into a viable dotcom (or even a non-viable dotcom, since these people don't care wether you make money as long as you pay for their services up front) you'll need some help. Lots of help. >>>

F Internet Magazine

F The Guardian

F MacUser

Paul Slater
Scoop

M Acrylic

B A case of mistaken identity means an incompetent newspaper reporter is sent to cover an African conflict, but somehow he secures a huge scoop

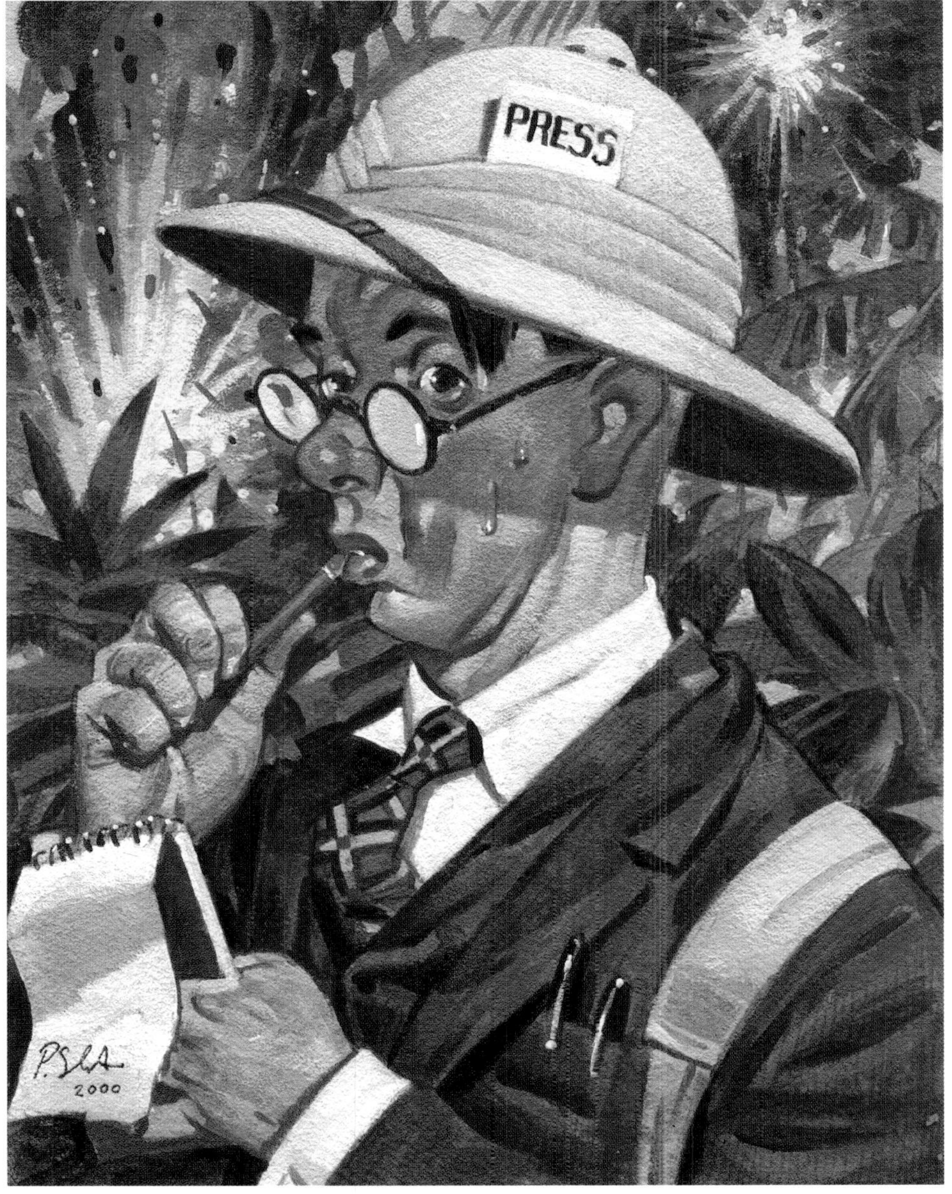

C Caroline Sallis

F Radio Times
RadioTimes

Andy Smith
Claridges
M Original art / digital
B Illustration of Claridges foyer

F Independent

Andy Smith
Five Letters
Beginning with B

M Original art / digital

B Make an image based on the alphabet

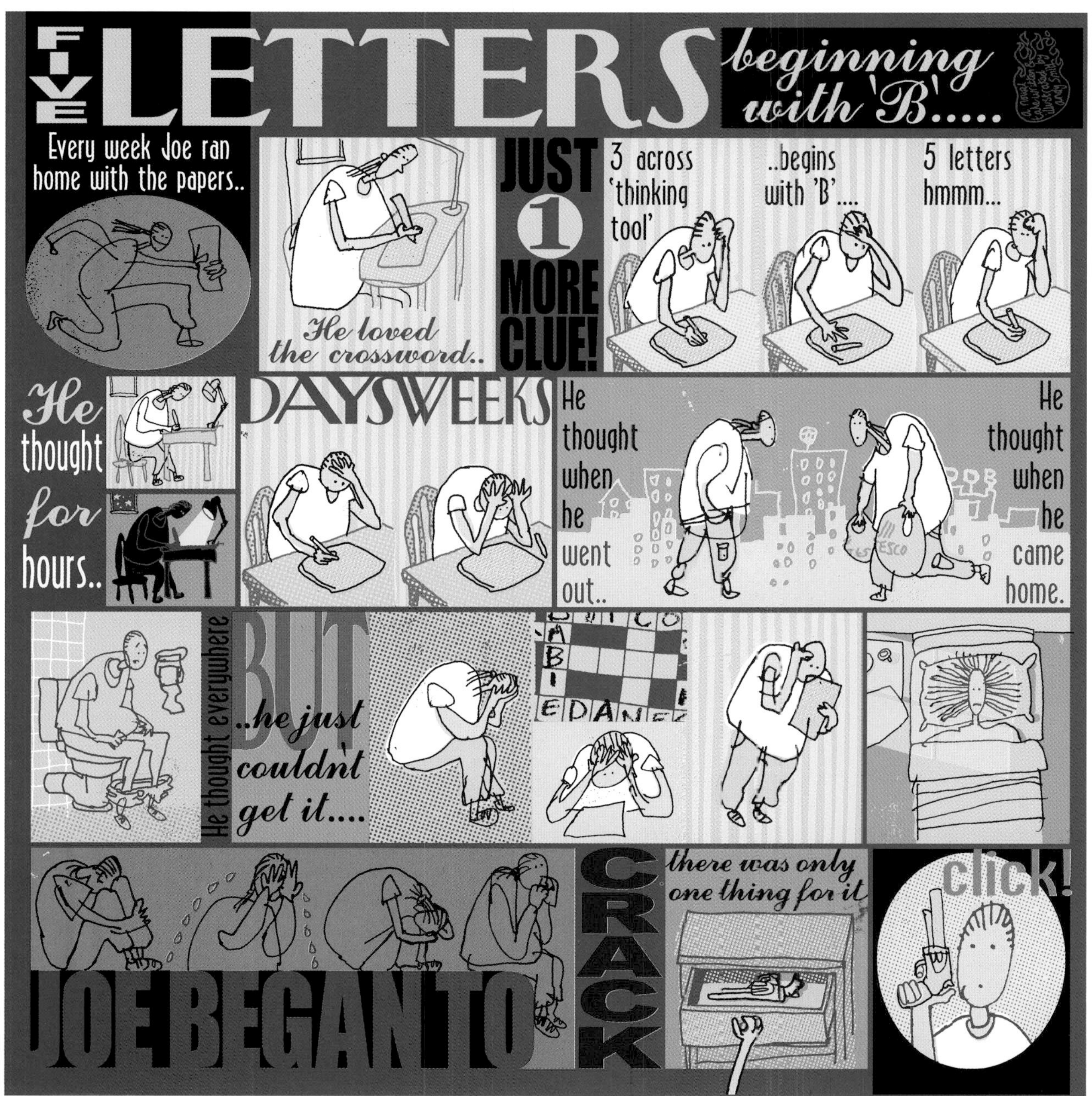

Simon Spilsbury

Airchaos

M Mixed media

B To represent summer holiday madness at airports

C Yasmina Jambresic

F Saturday Telegraph

David Tazzyman

Masai Warrior

M Original art / digital

B Drawing of a Masai warrior with technological gadgets to illustrate the third world's embracing new technologies

F Daily Telegraph

Peter Till
GM Food

M Pen and ink (line and wash)

B Illustrate an article on pros and cons of GM food

C Martin Colyer

F Reader's Digest

Nancy Tolford
T.V. Beauty

M Digital

B To illustrate an article praising the skills of television make-up artists

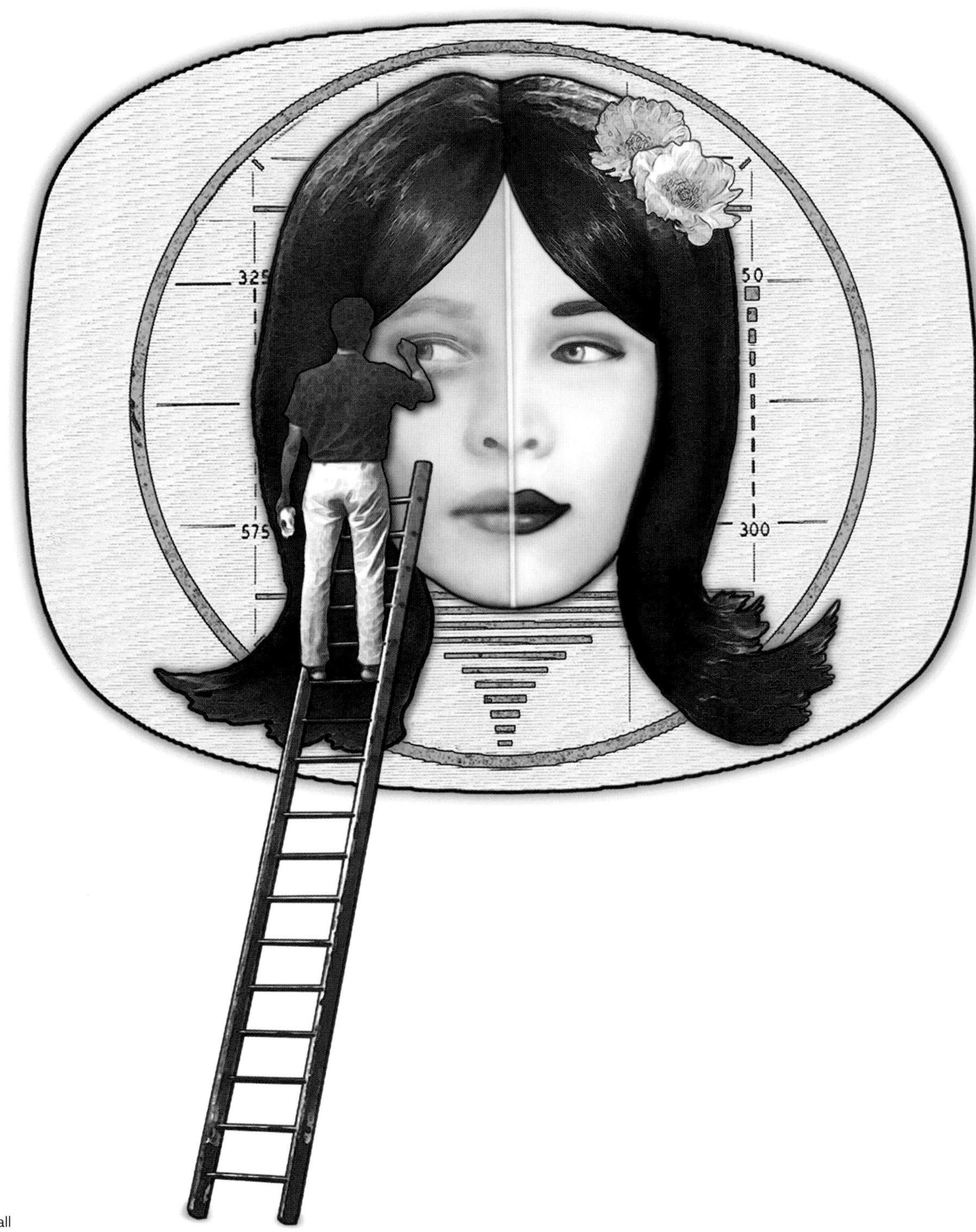

C Graham Ball

F The Times Magazine

Bob Venables
Election Victory for Berlusconi

M Alkyd

B After all his critics in the Italian press, Berlusconi wins, to prove his doubters wrong

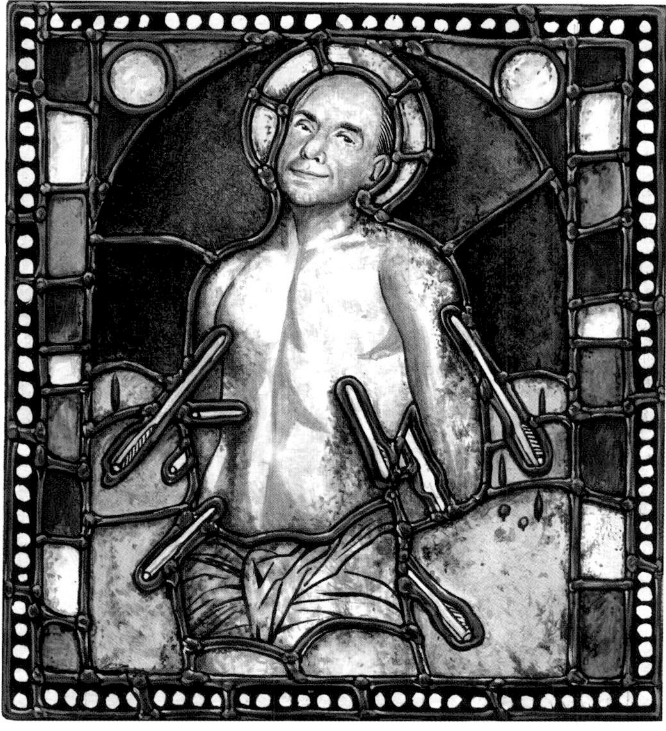

C John White

F Time Magazine

Helen Wakefield
Ian Rankin

M Paint, collage

B One of a series of caricatures of personalities who were questioned by readers

C Martin Colyer

F Reader's Digest

Helen Wakefield
Deadly Drug

M Paint, collage

B To illustrate article on heroin epidemic among young people

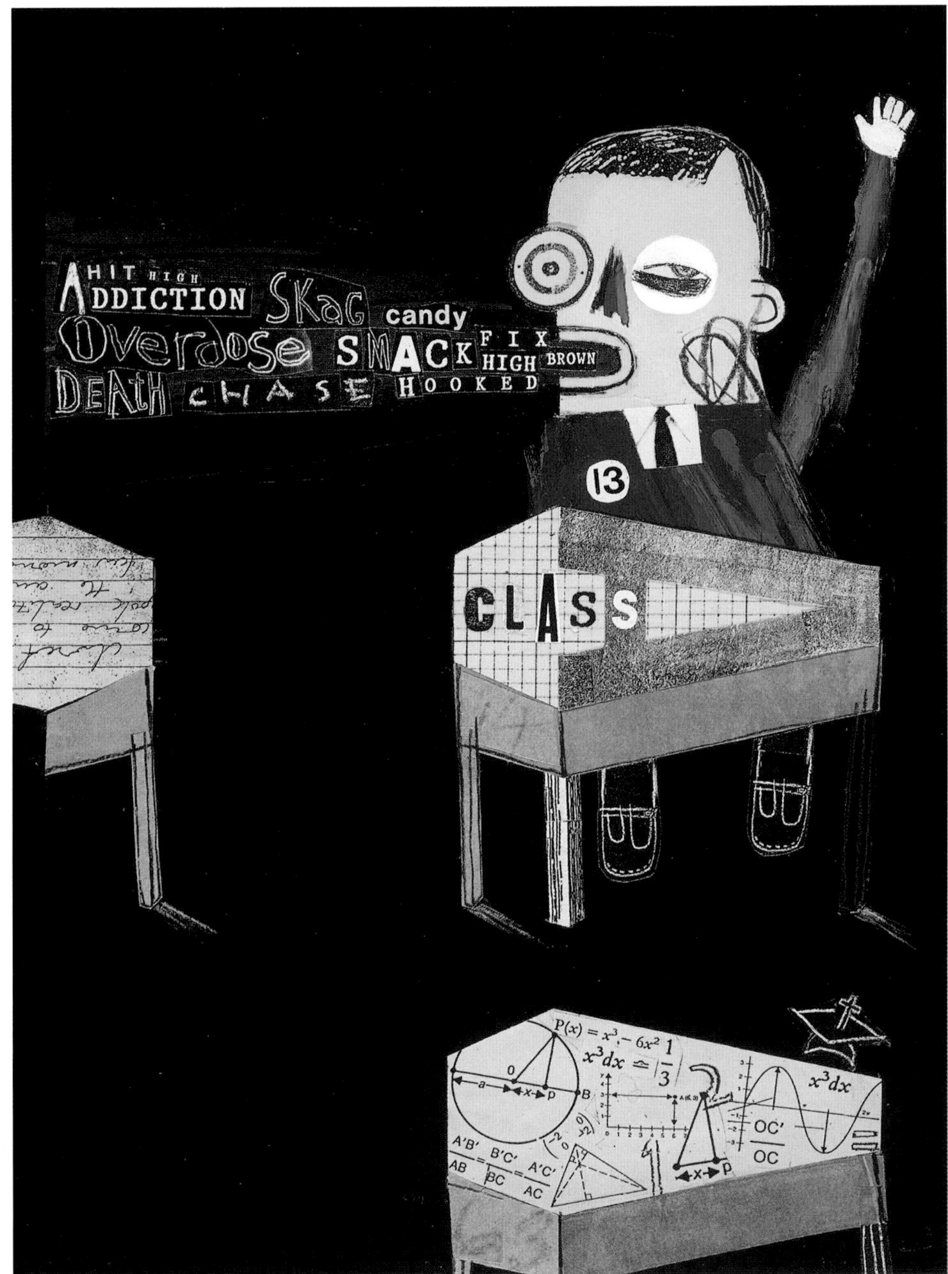

C Martin Colyer

F Reader's Digest

Paul Wearing

The Class of the Internet 1

M Digital

B Tech visionaries thought the internet would help bring rich and poor together. The truth so far is it's just pushing us further apart

The Class of the Internet 2

M Digital

B Illustrate feature about the growing class divide being created by the internet. Only 2% of the world population enjoys the benefit of the net

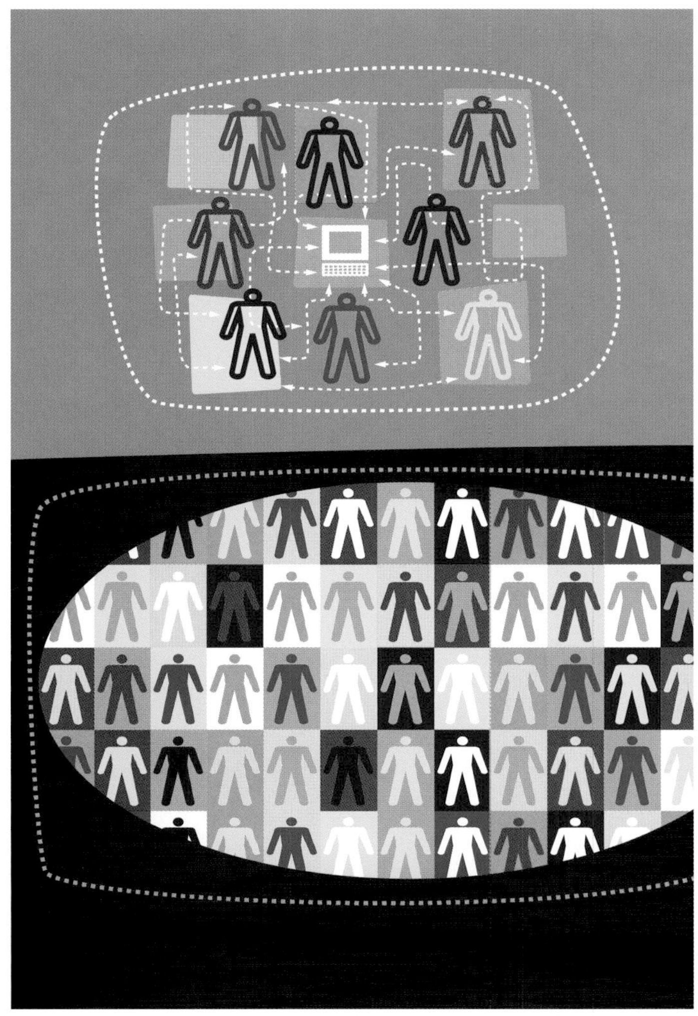

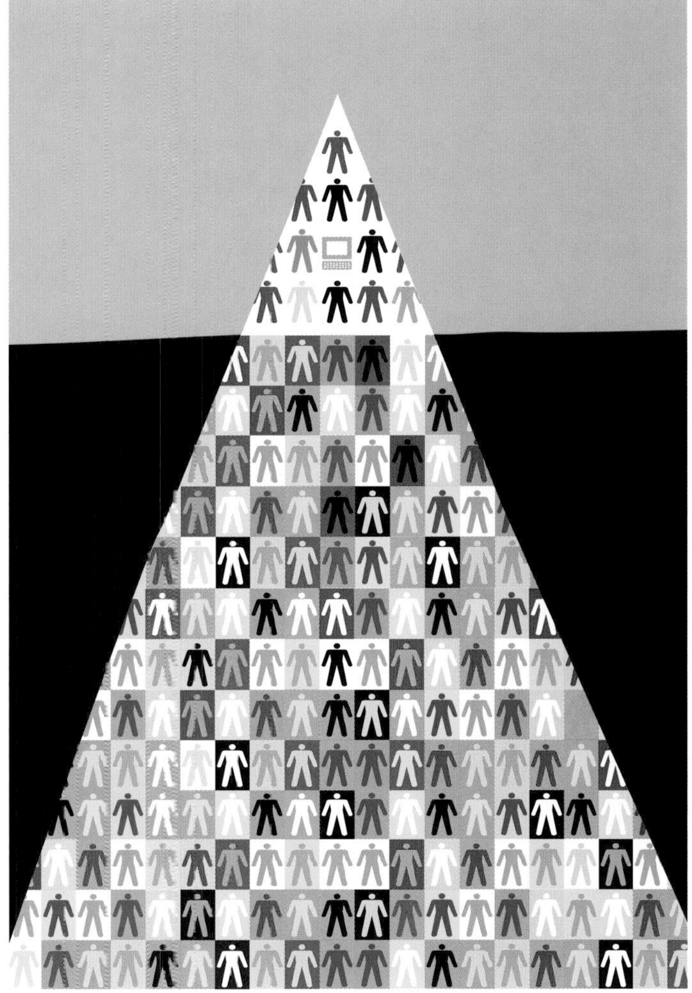

C Deanna Lowe
F Worth

C Deanna Lowe
F Worth

Paul Wearing

For Millionaires Only

M Digital

B Illustrate feature about how banks are rushing to provide online services for millionaires and changing the way affluent investors manage their assets

Surfing Safaris

M Digital

B The internet used to be a place to buy cheap plane tickets – now it's an invaluable tool for seeking out the world's luxury vacations

Retirement Strategy

M Digital

B Illustration for feature on retirement investments 'Don't Let a Lay-off Derail Your Retirement Savings Plan'

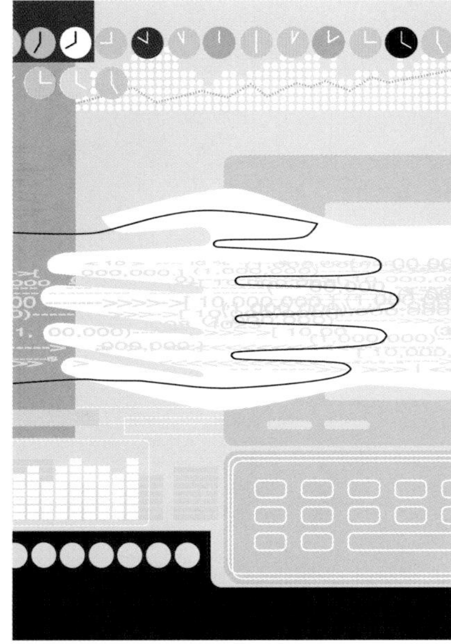

C Deanna Lowe

F Worth

C Deanna Lowe

F Worth

C Laura Riera

F Fidelity Focus

Editing Revolution

M Digital

B Double page spread for feature on new video editing software for the home

The Power of Personalisation

M Digital

B Illustrate feature about how e-tailers are attempting to customise and personalise their sites to individual customers

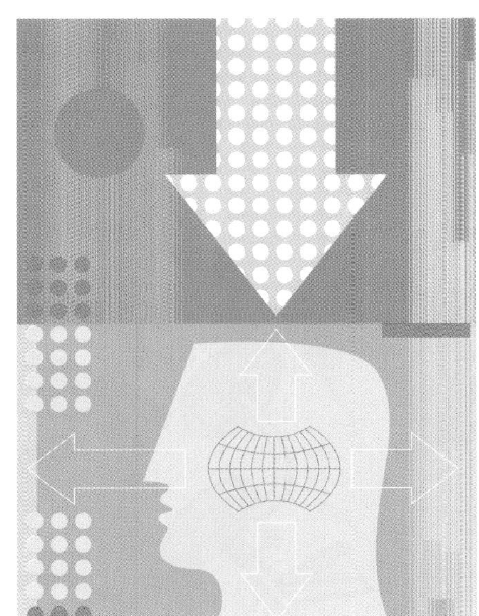

C Kristina De Mateo

F Sony Style

C Dennis McLeod

F Informix

Ian Whadcock
Value Creation in E-Commerce

M Digital

B Strategies used by e-com companies to create added value to their business – how do successful e-coms attract business interest, how do they create 'value' / increased stickiness to the dot com

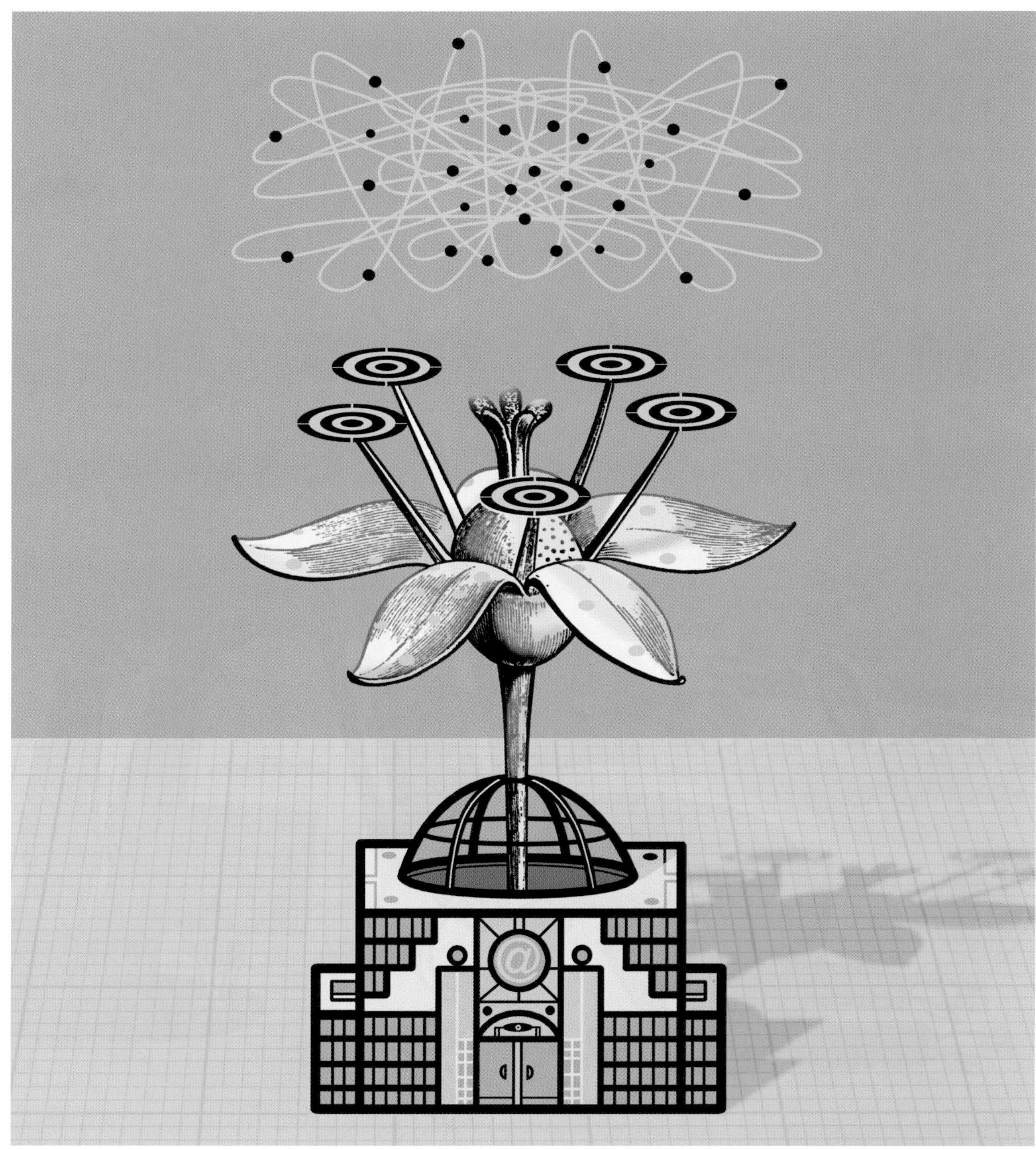

C Mike Lackersteen

F Esterson Lackersteen

Company Valuation / 'A Bird in the Bush...'

M Digital

B To provide a cover in the Mastering Investment series for the FT on the subject of how business valuations are achieved and comparisons made

C Hayley Ward

F Financial Times

Samantha Wilson
A Taste of the Suite Life

M Mixed media

B Illustration article on the new trend of holding a private get together in a hotel suite

C Sina Capaldo

F Mail on Sunday (for You Magazine)

Janet Woolley
East Ender's Dot Cotton is sent to prison

M Mixed media

B Soap illustration portraying Dot Cotton being sent to prison – Dot is guilt ridden over Ethel's death and deliberately doesn't turn up for court on a shoplifting charge

C Paul Smith

F Radio Times

RadioTimes

Jonathan Williams
Gimme Big Mac 'n' Fries To Go

M Digital

B If you plan to outlive everyone you know, end that fast food addiction!

C Amanda Scope

F Men's Health

BRIEF

Children's books
Gold award winner

Paul Hess

G Hungry, Hungry, Hungry

M Watercolour

B Front cover of a fully illustrated book for Malachy Doyle's poem

G

C Janice Thomson

F Anderson Press

Sarah Dyer
Five Little Fiends
M Mixed media
B Illustrations for a children's book titled 'Five Little Fiends'

Frances Cony
Cows
M Watercolour
B Open brief to illustrate two cow poems as a double page spread for a poetry anthology 'Hoddley Poddley'

C Sarah Odedina
F Bloomsbury

C Anna-Louise Billson
F Orchard Books

Cathy Gale
All Your Own Teeth
(double spread
from book)

M Gouache, collage

B 'Have fun!' Young boy (Stewart) loves painting, never seen a real animal so goes to the jungle to find one to draw...

C Sarah Odedina

F Bloomsbury
Children's Books

Luana Geiger
Red

M Gouache

B One of a series of images to illustrate a children's book about Brazilian Indian myths

Robin Heighway-Bury (B)
Who Built the Pyramid?

M Digital/mixed media

B The story of the building of a pyramid and all those responsible for the process

(B)

F Cosac & Naify

C Beth Aves

F Walker Books

Adrian Johnson
Nonsense: Art & Bob

M Digital

B An a-z picture book of nonsense names for boys

Karin Littlewood
Ellie

M Watercolour & gouache

B To illustrate the story of a little girl who finds a kitten on the beach

C Cecile Goyette

F Penguin Putnam

C Anna Billson

F Orchard Books

Richard Johnson

S The Laughing Troll
M Acrylic
B To illustrate the story of 'The Three Billy Goats Gruff', the Troll waits for a bigger meal

The Children's School
M Acrylic
B To depict the setting for the revised story of 'The Enormous Turnip'

C Mishti Chatteri
F Mantra Publishing

C Mishti Chatteri
F Mantra Publishing

Anne Wilson
Noah Builds His Ark

M Printing inks and collage

B To illustrate children's book 'Noah's Ark' – full colour picture book, all inside spreads and cover

C Janet Slingsby
Del Tucker

F Tuckerslingsby
Chronicle

book **images**

Jason Ford

S The Third Man

M Gouache

B Audio cassette sleeve cover image of Graham Greene's novel

S

C Matt Bookman

F BBC Radio Collection

BBC RADIO COLLECTION

Geoff Grandfield

Tinker, Tailor, Soldier, Spy

Smiley's People

The Russia House

M Pastel

B Audio cassette sleeve cover image of John Le Carré's novel. Part of a series of five

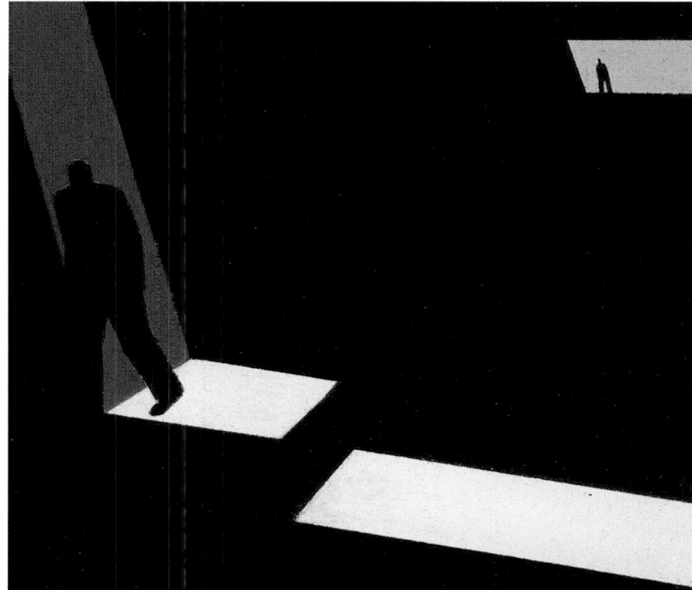

C Matt Bookman

F BBC Radio Collection

BBC RADIO COLLECTION

Nick Hardcastle

B A Death in the Family

M Pen and ink

B To illustrate a scene from each short story (Great Crime Stories, Volume 4)

The Obituarist's Outing (Great Crime Stories, Volume 4)

The Stoke Parva Murder (Great Crime Stories, Volume 1)

Levinson's Victim (Great Crime Stories, Volume 1)

B

C Joe Whitlock Blundell

F Folio Society

David Holmes
Primrose Hill
Remembered

M Watercolour, crayon

B Illustrate book cover

C Myra

F Chalk Farm Library
(for The Friends of
Chalk Farm Library)

Mark Hudson
The Lord of the Rings
M Digital
B Tolkien's narrative in a single image which could be divided into seven separate connecting covers. Each section containing only information relevant to its corresponding episode

Suzanna Hubbard
'Romance' Robert Louis Stevenson
M Watercolour
B One of 56 illustrations to illustrate a book of love poetry

C Matt Bookman
F BBC Radio Collection

BBC RADIO COLLECTION

C Kate Shearman
F Orion Publishing

Debra McFarlane

The Bishop

M Etching

B To illustrate 'Anton Chekhov – Short Stories'

The Lady with the Dog

C Joe Whitlock Blundell

F The Folio Society

Ian Pollock
Unreal

M Watercolour, ink, gouache

B Cover illustration for a collection of short stories by Paul Jennings

Rachel Ross
Father Brown

M Gouache

B Audio cassette sleeve cover image illustrating various adventures of the famous French sleuth

C George Dale

F Penguin Books (Australia)

C Matt Bookman

F BBC Radio Collection

BBC RADIO COLLECTION

Ian Whadcock
Improving Your Memory

M Digital

B To illustrate how various object / number association techniques can be used to improve your ability to remember things and increase the potential of your memory

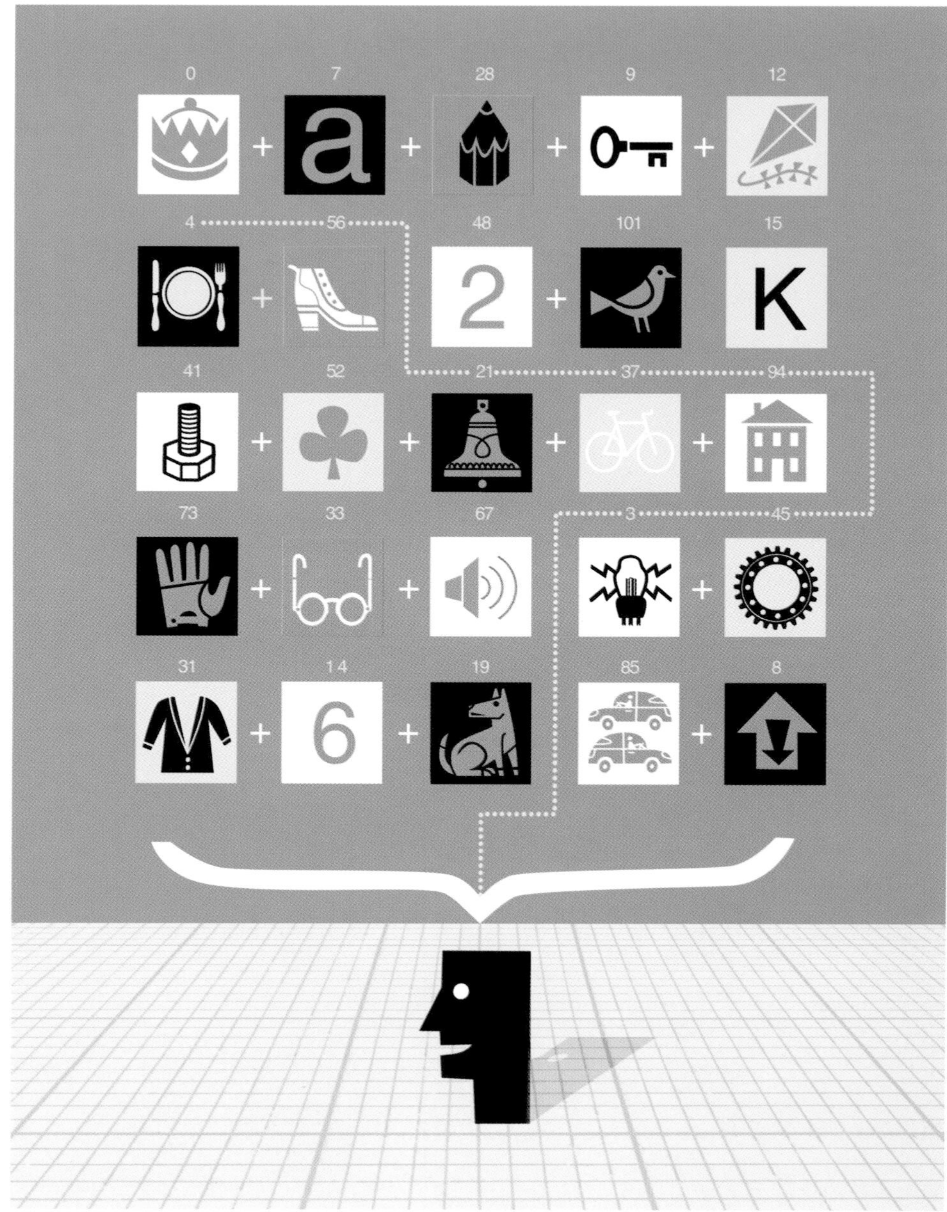

C Tim Foster

F Duncan Baird Publishing / Reader's Digest

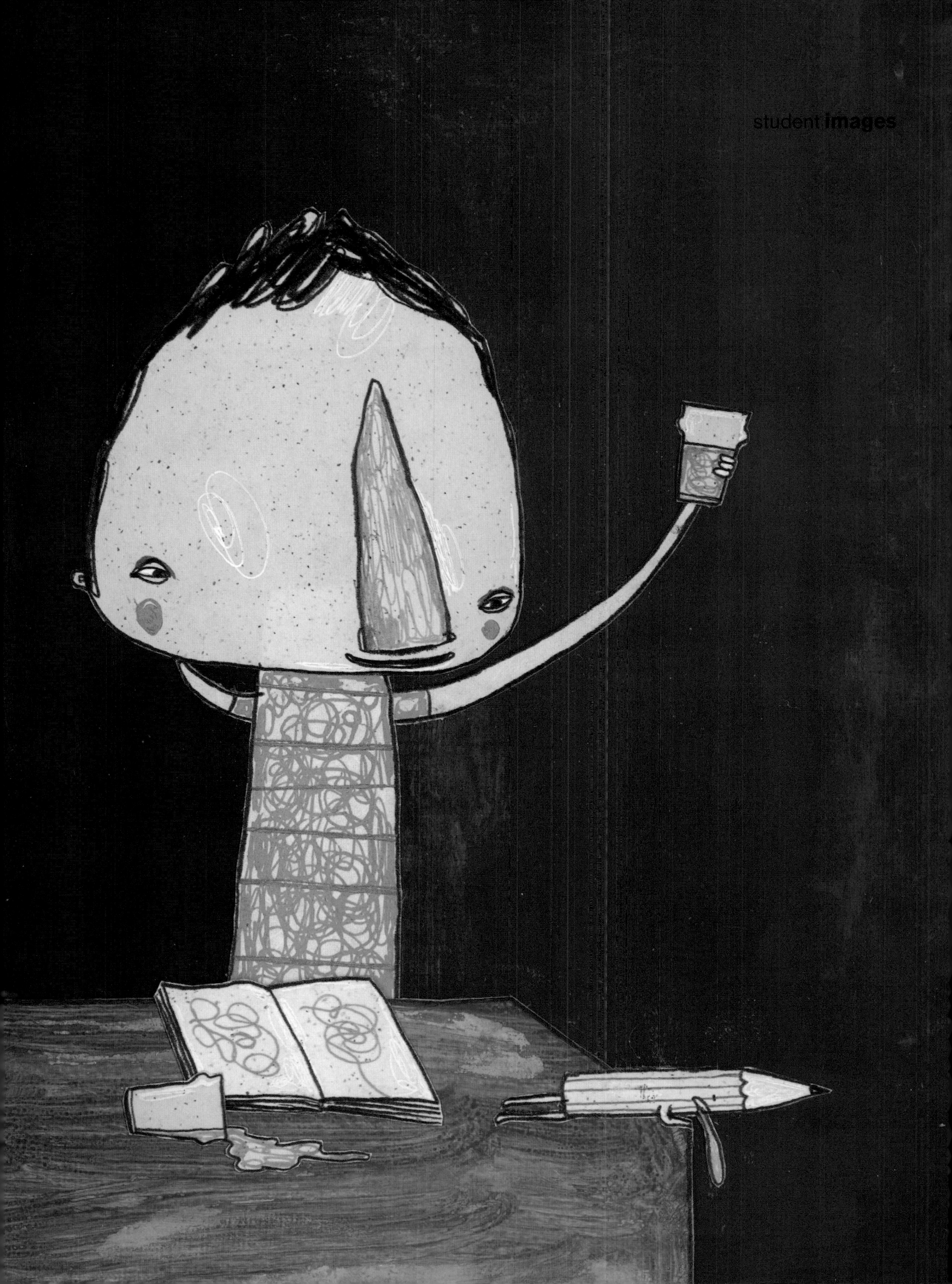

Laura Collins
Lympstone, Devon
2001

M Acrylic, watercolour

B Illustration from a small book called 'We Went on the Train to Find the Sea' (one book in a series about relationships and love)

Chris Cowdrill
Cafeteria – Pub
M Mixed media
B Personal developmental work

Luzette Donohue
Reminisce

M Digital

B Provide an illustration that challenges the viewer's perception of digital art

Claire Hammond
Nine to Five
M Newspaper, oil & acrylic
B Produce a double page illustration for the article 'Work Ethic vs Play Ethic' in the Observer Life Magazine

Tina Gander
The Functions of the Tree
M Watercolour, gouache, collage
B To design a poster, aimed at children, to describe the functions of a tree

Julia Hammond
Tainted Realm

M Pen and ink
(line and wash)

B The front cover of Aldous Huxley's 'Brave New World' is illustrated for a recent project. It shows a native witnessing the devastating effects of pollution

Gina Holley
Gulliver
M Mixed media
B An illustration from Gulliver's Travels

Katy Jackson

Oscar Wilde

M Mixed media

B Narrative piece on Oscar Wilde showing him at the end of his literary career

Underwater Woman

M Mixed media

B Atmospheric piece showing figure within an environment

Akiko Kamae
Hue & Pants, Bruce
M Digital
B Character studies

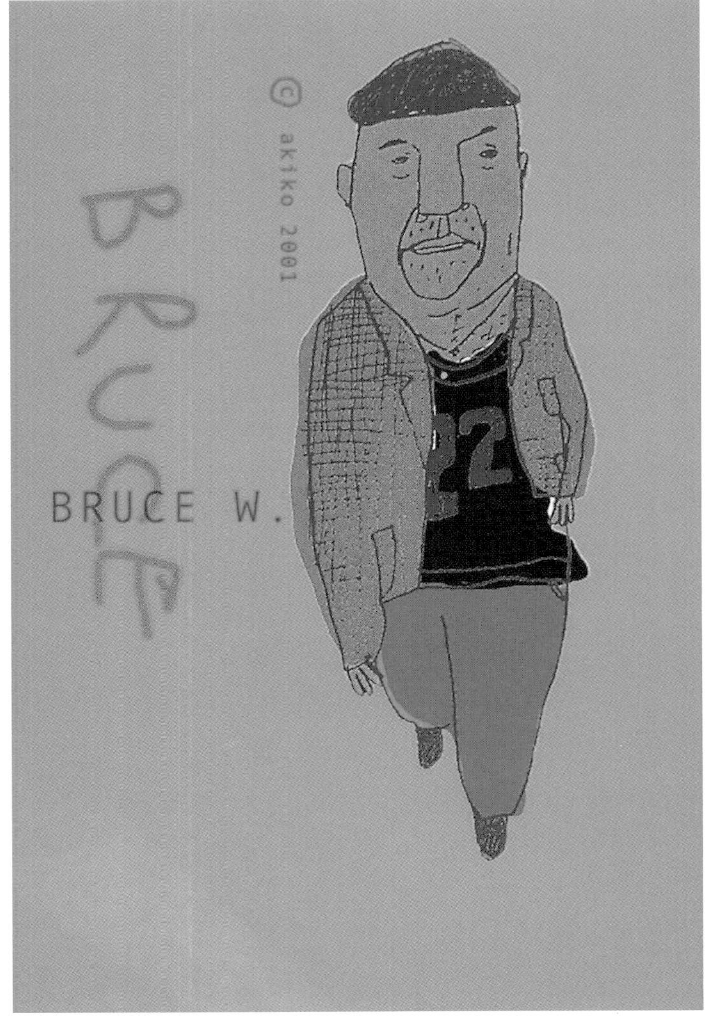

Samantha Meredith
A Wonderful Time Was Had By All

M Mixed media

B A page from my children's book entitled 'Boy's Birthday'

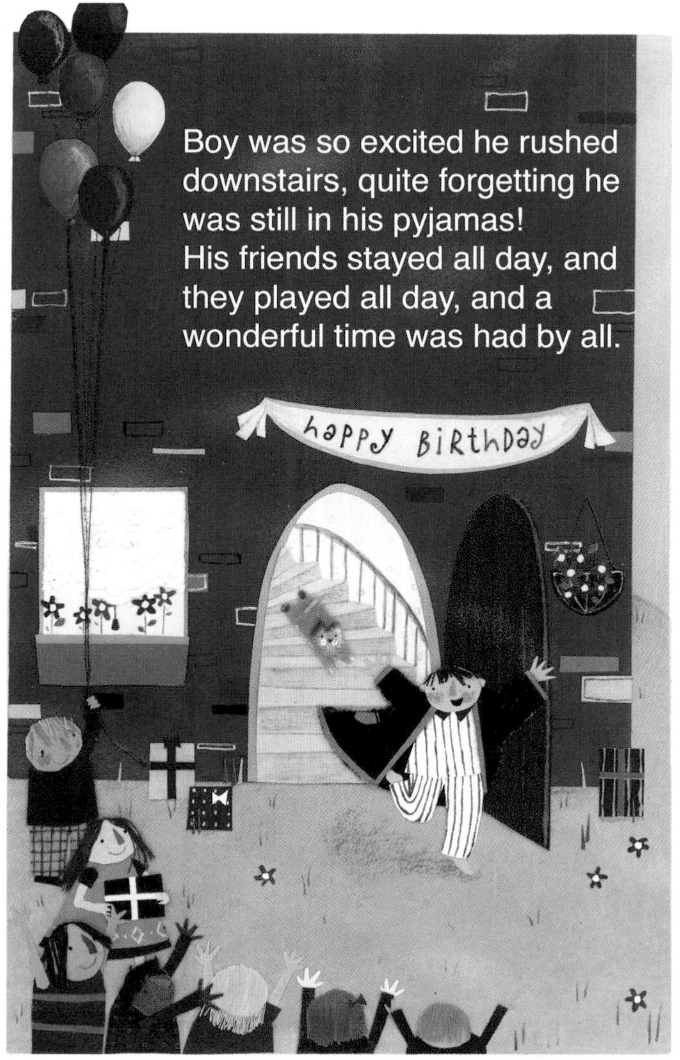

Boy was so excited he rushed downstairs, quite forgetting he was still in his pyjamas!
His friends stayed all day, and they played all day, and a wonderful time was had by all.
happy BiRthDay

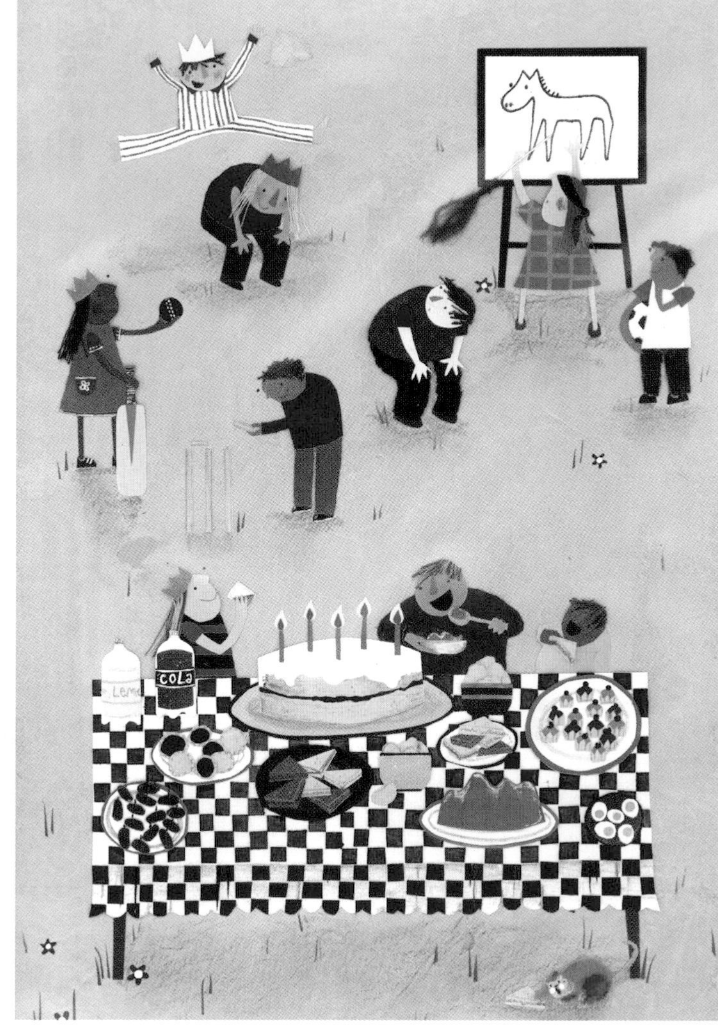

Jessica Mikhail

Get Stuck in a Book
M Collage
B Personal project: to stimulate children to read. Suitable for posters, bookmarks etc

The Cosmic Angel
M Collage
B Personal project: children's storybook 'The Cosmic Angel'

Shelle Pugh

(B) Air Servicemen's Memorial

M Mixed media: digitally enhanced

B Narrative image focussing on an airman's memories in air combat

(B)

Finlay Ralph
Too Much, Too Young

M Ink

B Accompanying illustration for an article on the adverse effects of stress on children – University project

Steve Shipley
Irish Eyes

M Mixed media

B Produce a series of portraits for the novel 'Tis' by Frank McCourt

Julia Staite
Bull in a China Shop

M Mixed media

B Create an image depicting an animal saying for an exhibition aimed at children aged 5 to 14

Dominic Trevett
Number Trail

M Digital

B Design a poster which would encourage a child to count numbers. This poster should be suitable for a primary school wall

F Project set by Surrey Institute of Art & Design

James Wakelin
Michael Flatley –
Lord of the Dance

M Acrylic
B Self-promotional

FOR HIRE

Unpublished
Gold award winner

Russell Cobb

G The New Coffee Works

M Acrylic

B To produce a series of unique and collectable postcards designed to heighten awareness of the illustrator's work. No. 9 based around the theme of coffee

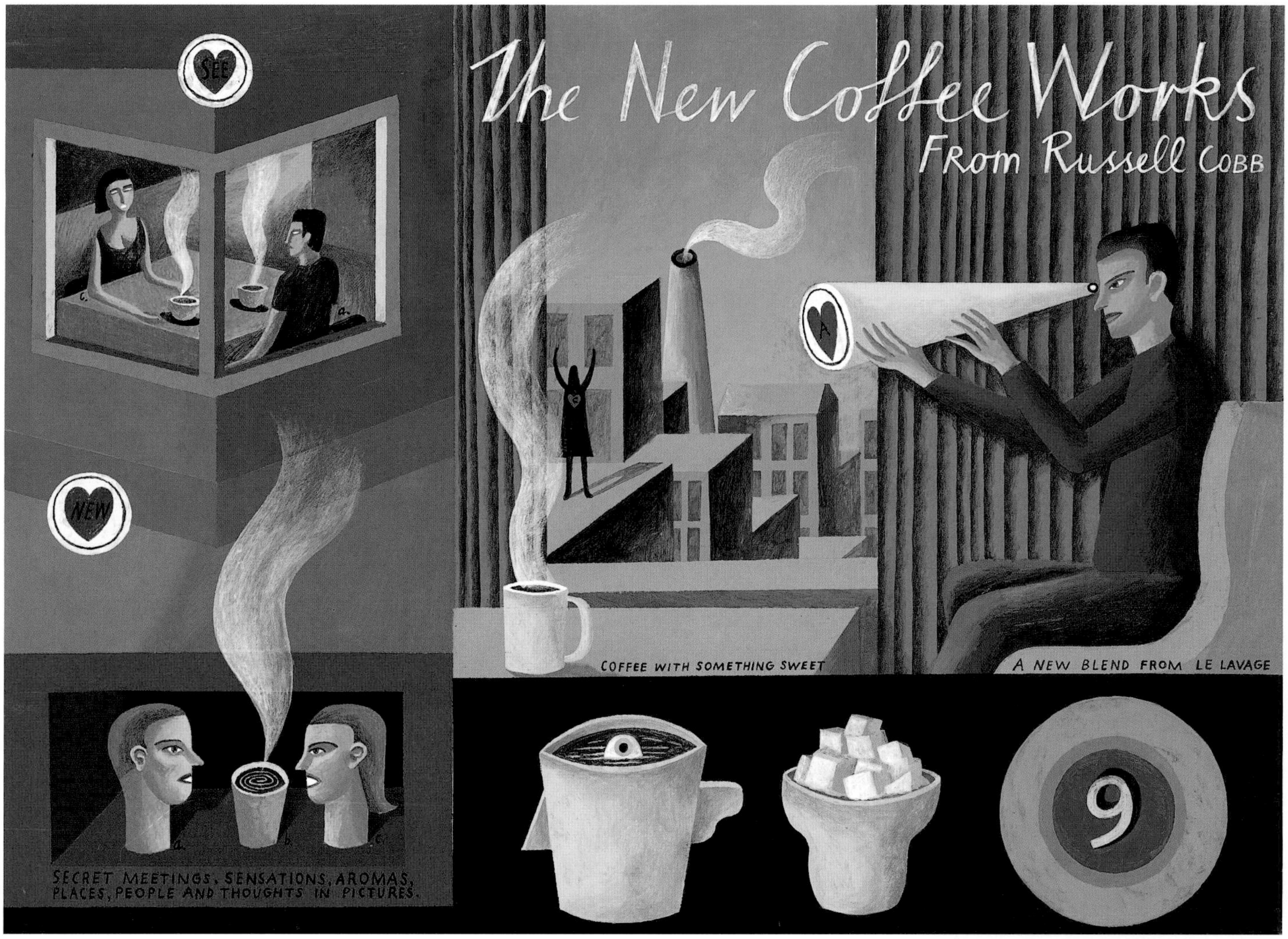

G

A. Richard Allen
Picnicking Kong
M Ink & digital
B Self promotional piece – speculative cover image for the New Yorker Magazine. Produced May 2001

David Bimson
Peace of Mind

M Acrylic, found surfaces

B To illustrate a seven framed sequential narrative, to accompany a personal poem

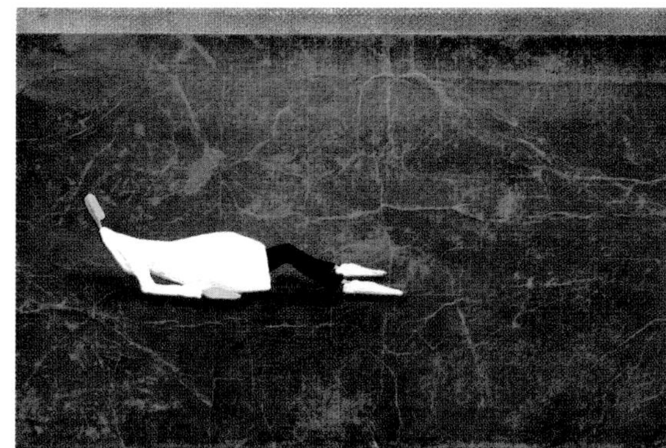

Michael Bramman

3rd of July –
Coral Gables

M Acrylic

B Promotional

Southern Climes

M Acrylic

B Promotional

Lizzie Buckmaster
Patron Saint of Messages

M Box construction with collage and assemblage

B From a series of Patron Saints. An exploration to push the boundaries of collage, making it more 3-dimensional

Paul Burgess

Sit!

M Collage

B Self promotional piece – one of a series, juxtaposing pets with architecture

Jane B

M Mixed media

B Self promotional piece about Jane Birkin and Serge Gainsbourg

Russell Cobb

The New 7 Series Transport Works

M Acrylic

B To produce a series of unique and collectable postcards designed to heighten awareness of the illustrator's work

New Inflatable Hair

M Acrylic

B One of a series of images based on the theme of boxed novelty gifts ideal for modern life

Vitamin Cobb No. 15

The Shampoo Works No. 12

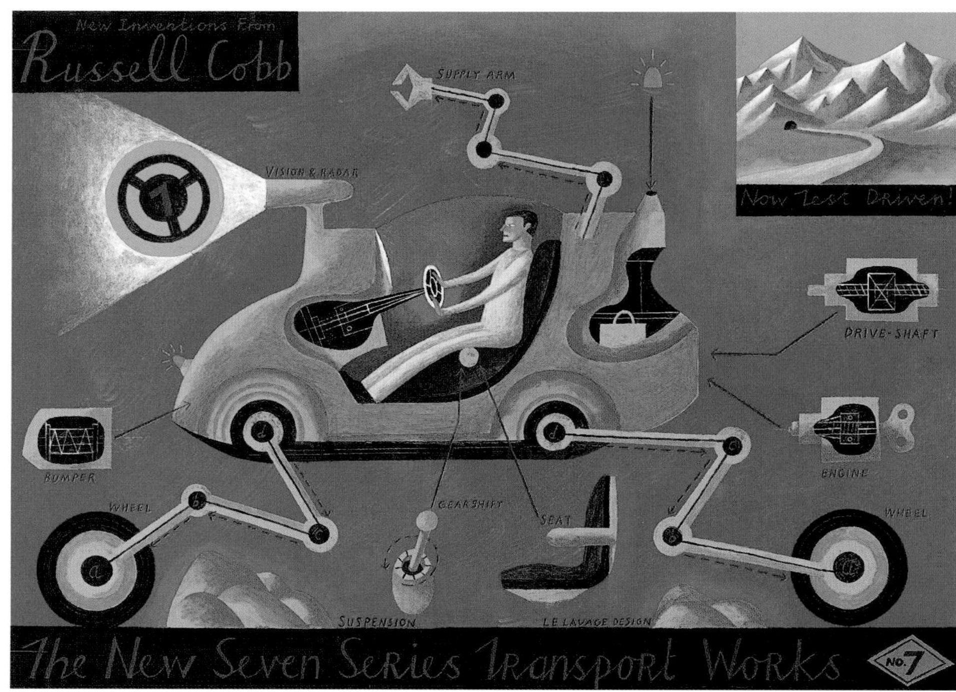

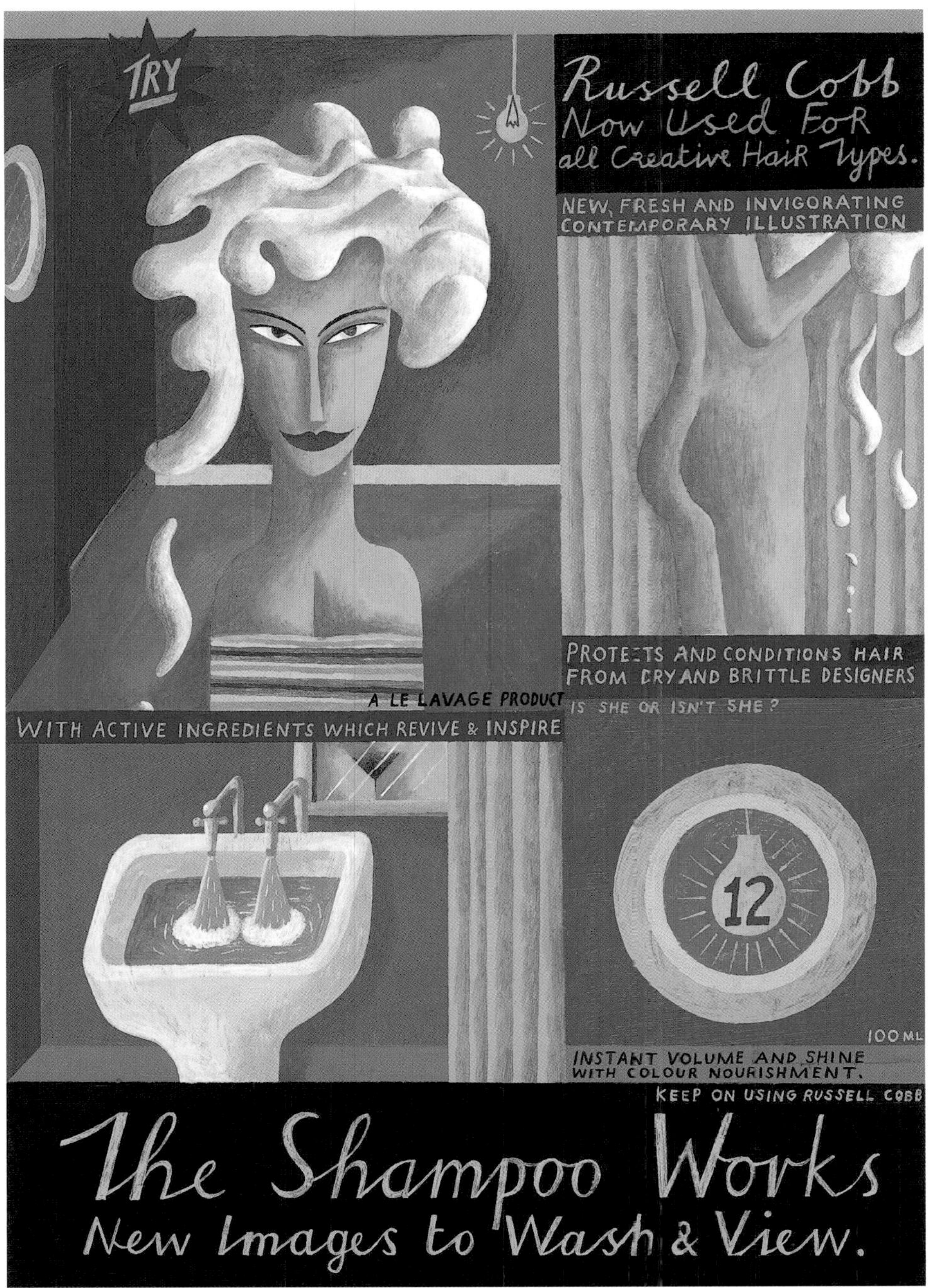
TRY
Russell Cobb
Now Used For
all Creative Hair Types.
NEW, FRESH AND INVIGORATING
CONTEMPORARY ILLUSTRATION
PROTECTS AND CONDITIONS HAIR
FROM DRY AND BRITTLE DESIGNERS
A LE LAVAGE PRODUCT
IS SHE OR ISN'T SHE?
WITH ACTIVE INGREDIENTS WHICH REVIVE & INSPIRE
12
100 ML
INSTANT VOLUME AND SHINE
WITH COLOUR NOURISHMENT.
KEEP ON USING RUSSELL COBB
The Shampoo Works
New Images to Wash & View.

Russell Cobb

The New Test Works

M Acrylic

B To produce a series of unique and collectable postcards designed to heighten awareness of the illustrator's work. No. 11 based on the theme of testing

New DIY Air Conditioning

M Acrylic

B One of a series of images based on the theme of boxed novelty gifts ideal for modern life

Animated Inventions

M Acrylic

B One of a series of images based on the theme of moving parts

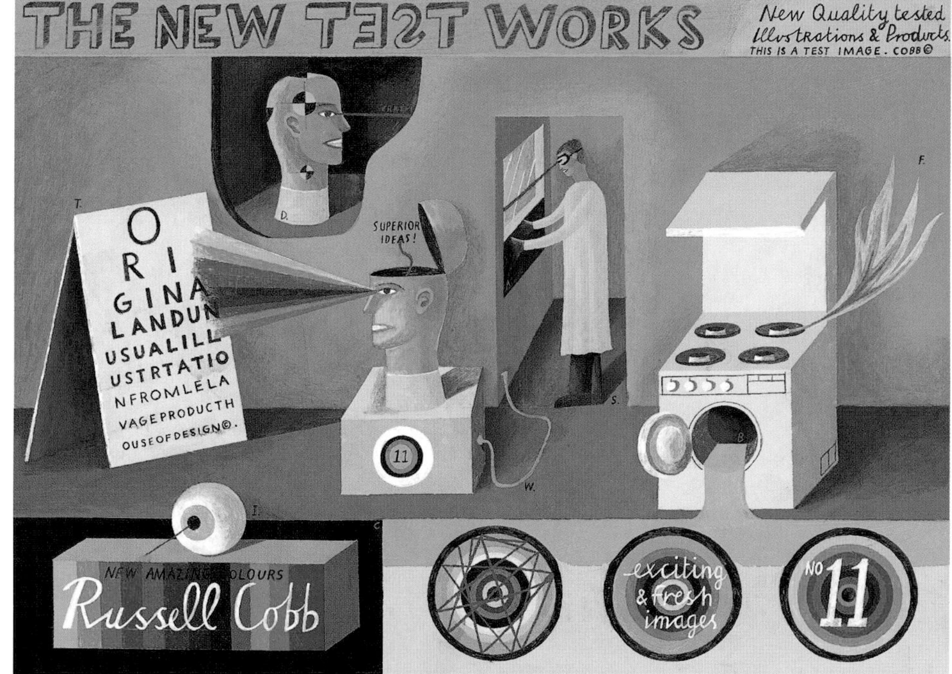

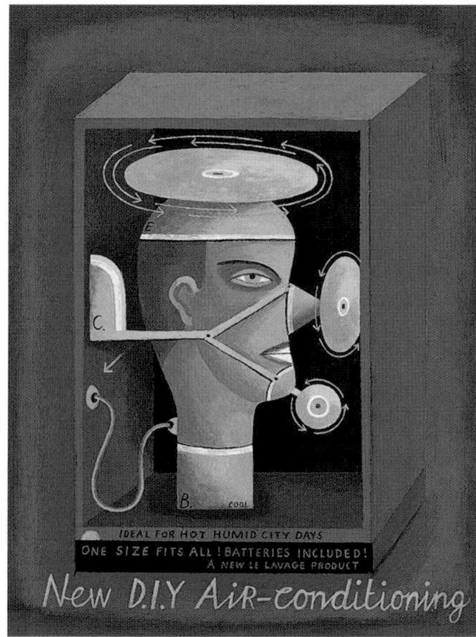

Brigid Collins

A Page of Love
(Golden Chamber)

M Mixed media

B An exploration of new materials, using poetry and dreams as a catalyst. Natural forms also carry symbolic meaning

A Page of Love
(Dark With Hope)

M Mixed media

B This piece is intended to appear to have been ripped from a larger volume, suggesting its place as part of an ongoing story

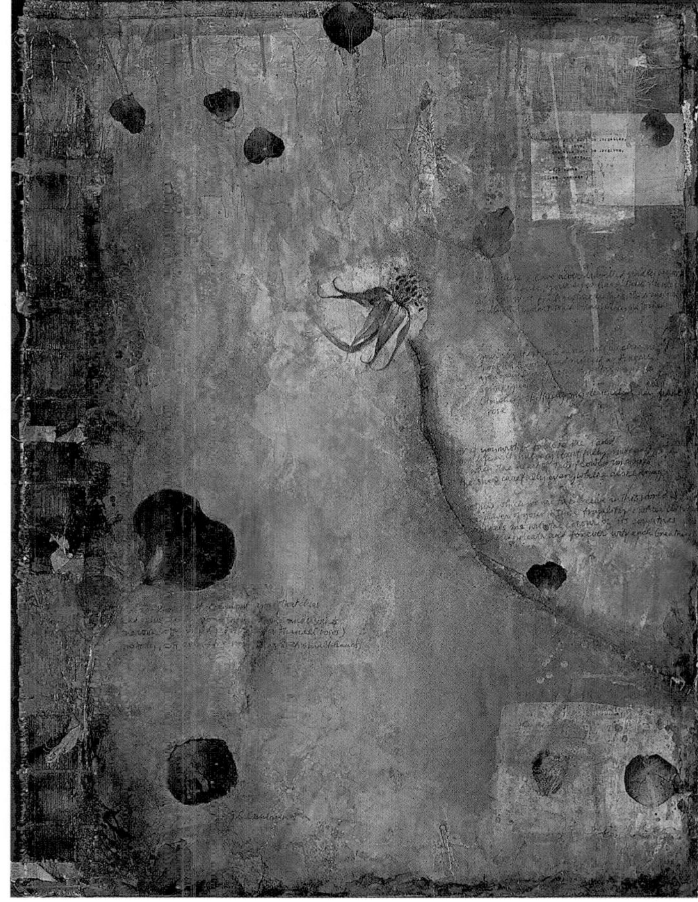

Charlotte Fiona Combe

Learning to Love

M Mixed media

B Speculative editorial piece for self promotion, experimenting with new technique to create a fresh and contemporary feel

Women with wings... do you believe in fairies?

M Mixed media

B Speculative editorial piece on women who believe in fairies. For self-promotion, experimenting with new technique to create a fresh and contemporary feel

Charlotte Fiona Combe
The Mistress of Spices
M Mixed media
B Speculative book cover for self promotion, experimenting with new technique

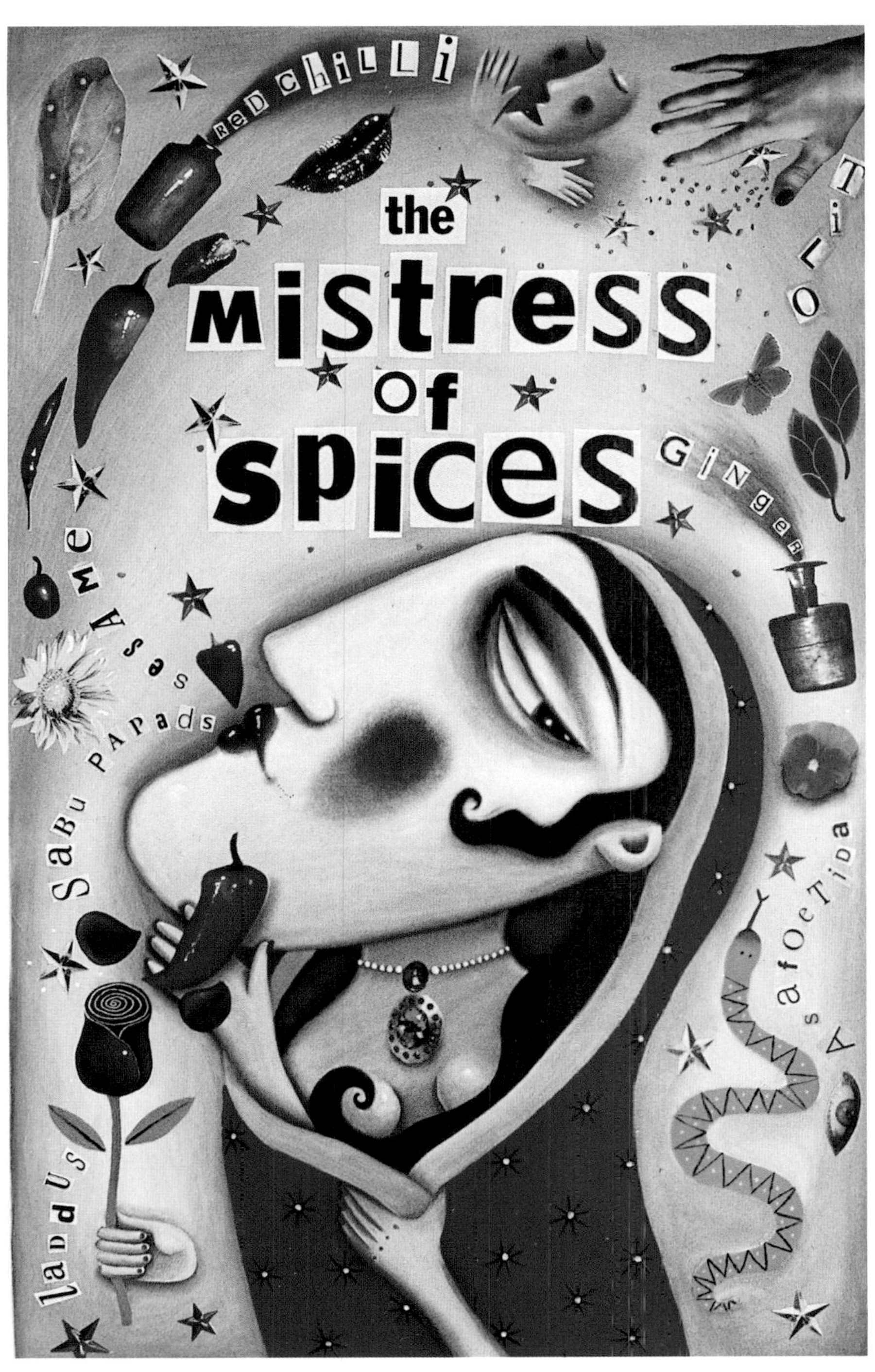

Georgia Denby
Squeeze!
M Mixed media
B Self promotional work

Benita Denny
Oppression
M Digital
B My intention was to make an illustration suitable for editorial use. This is one of a series of illustrations about hierarchies

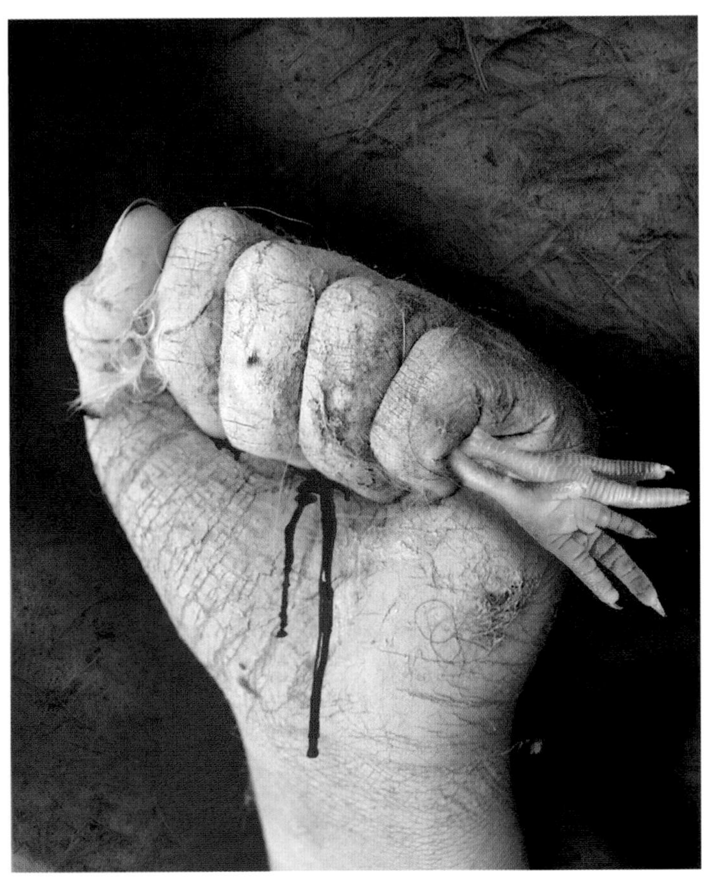

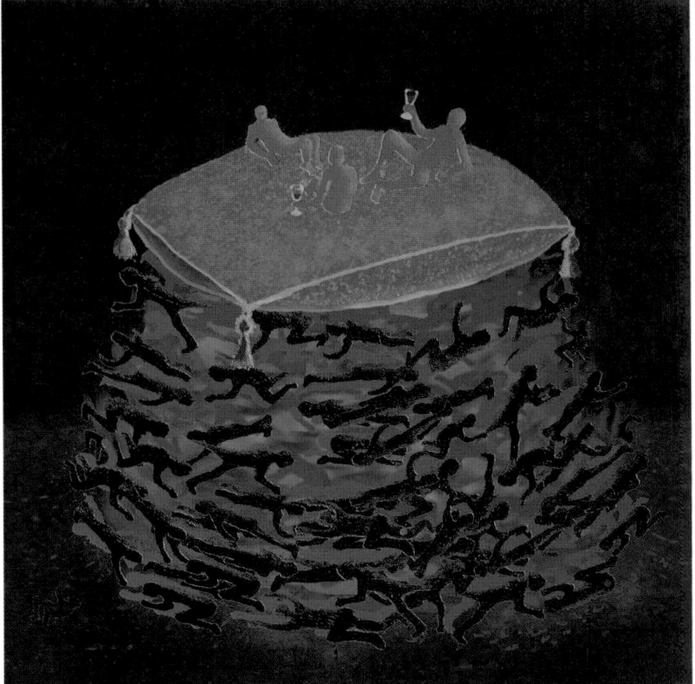

Alex Di Silvestro
Untitled
M Digital
B Poster/page for beachwear or travel advert, intended clients: Benetton Group and Club Med

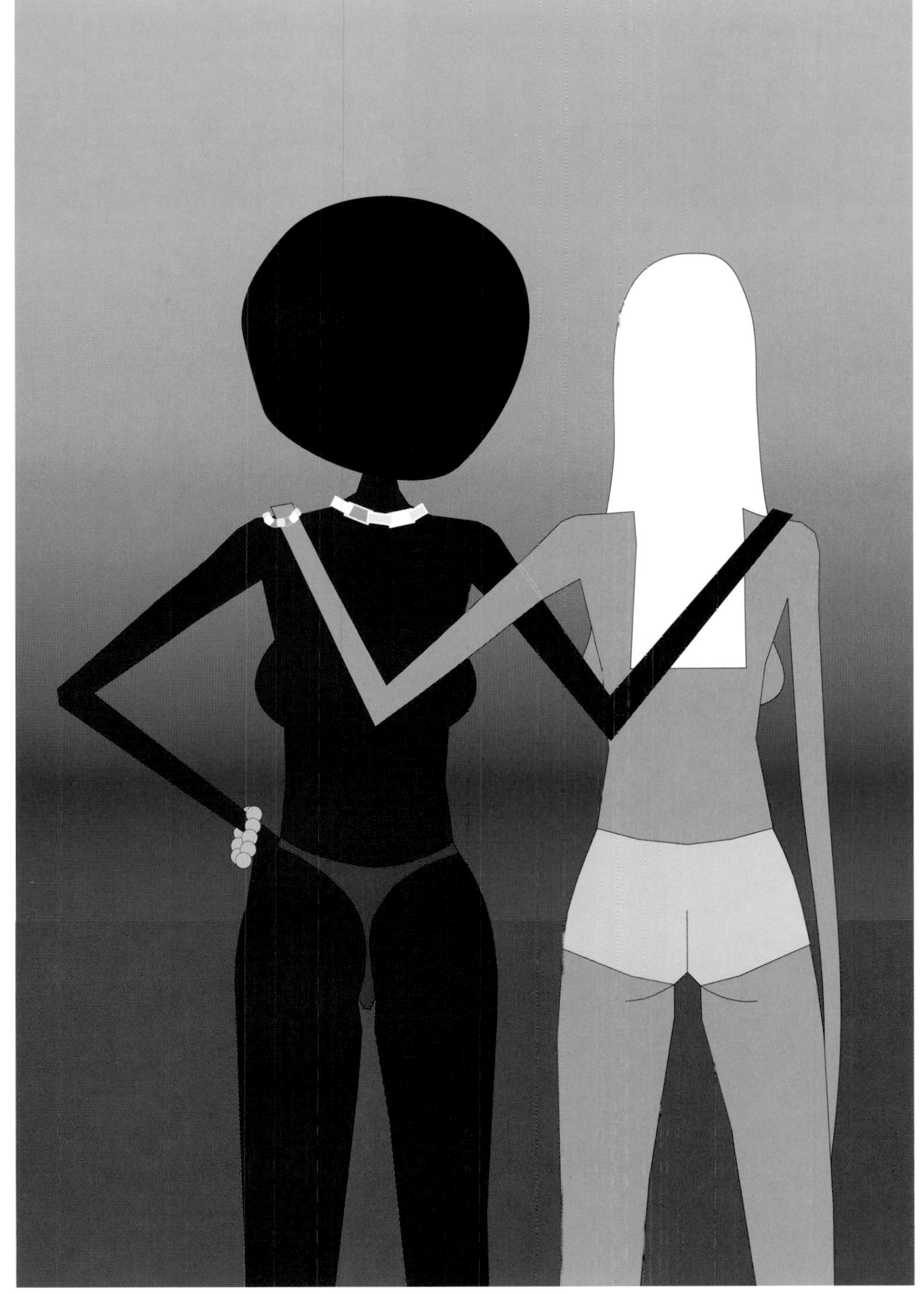

Willi Gray

Bacon

M Collage, paint, digital

B Experimental work for a food magazine

Migraine

M Collage, paint, digital

B Experimental work from a series on personal afflictions

Insomnia

Baldness

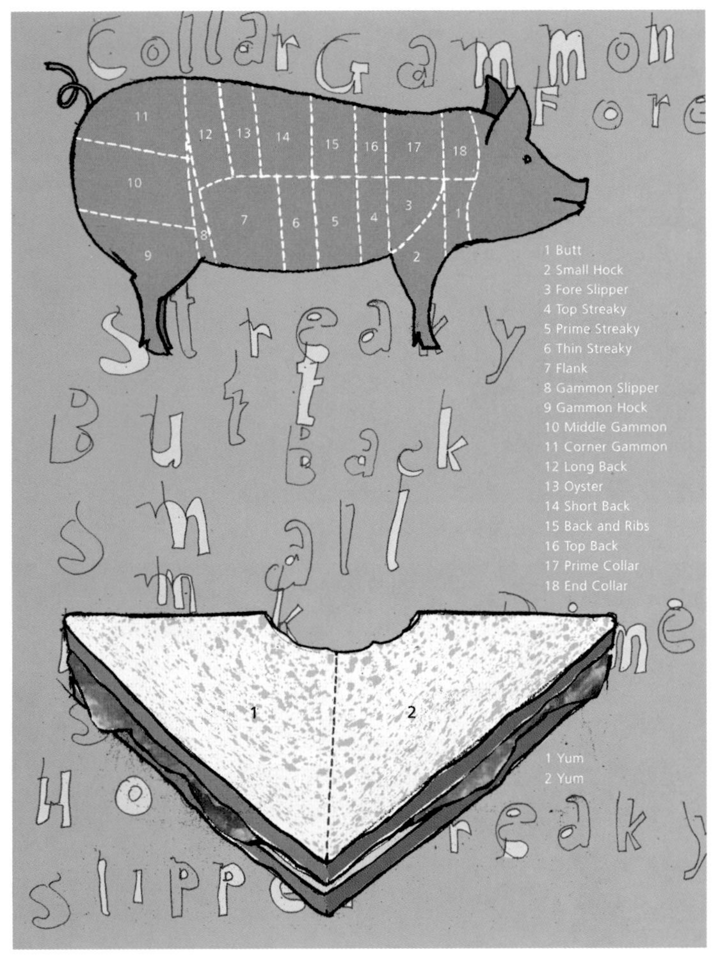

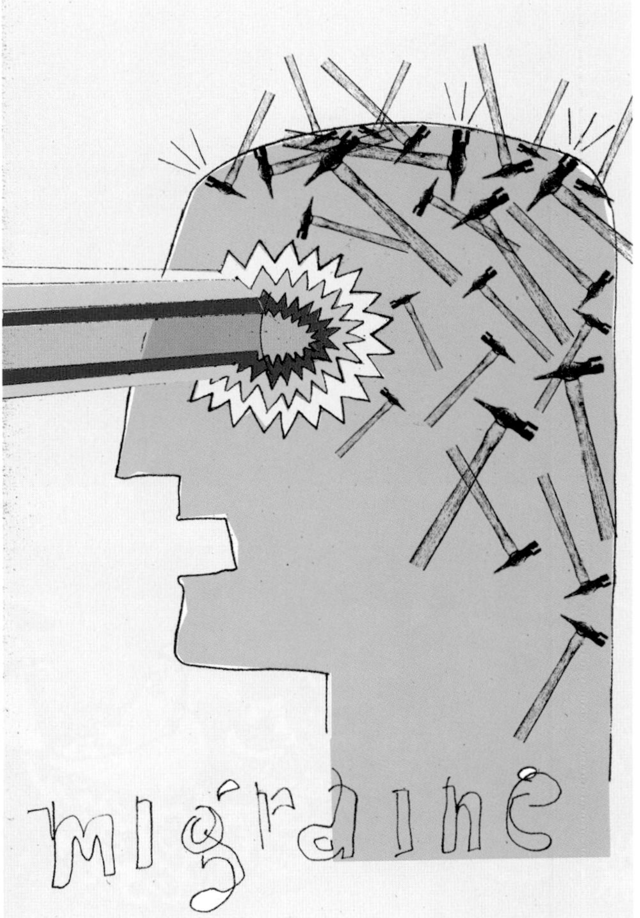

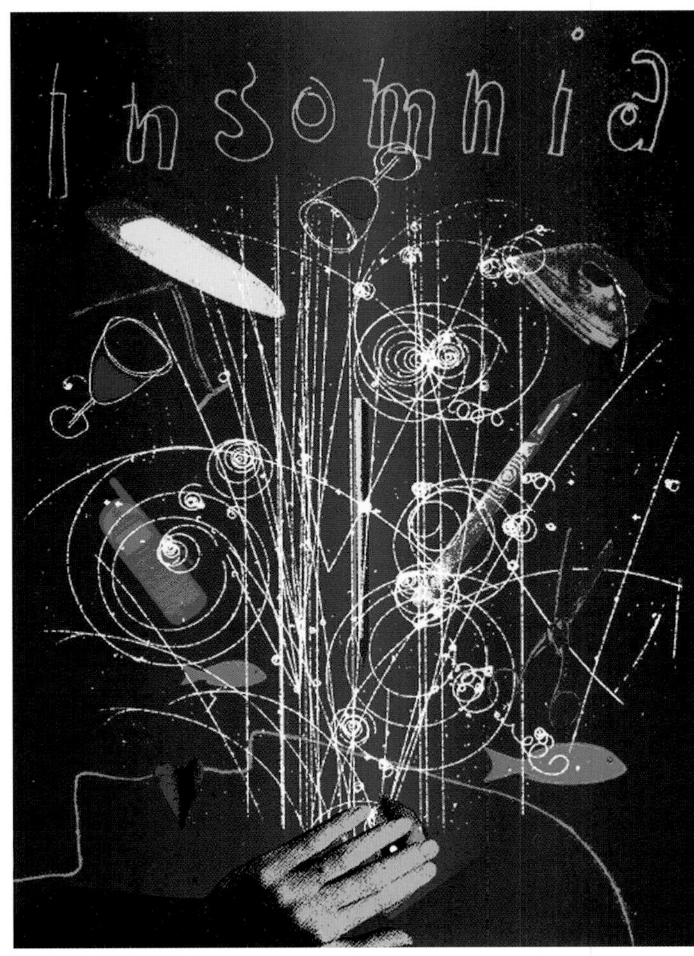
insomnia

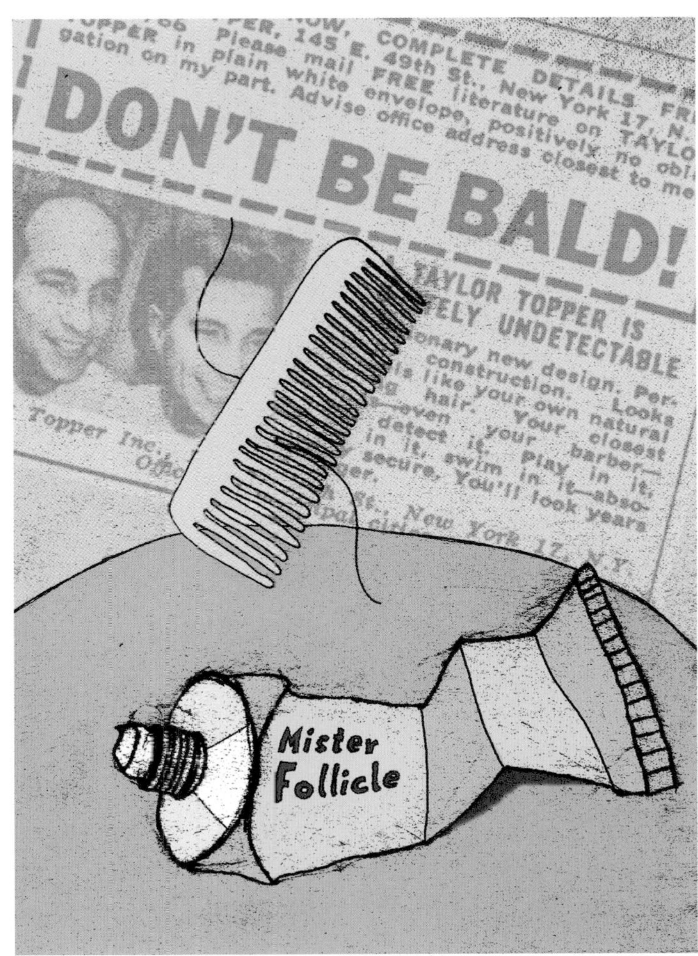
DON'T BE BALD!
TAYLOR TOPPER IS
UNDETECTABLE
Mister
Follicle

Brian Grimwood

Sketches from Spain
M Digital
B Self promotional

Charlie Parker
M Digital
B Self promotional

Peter Gudynas
'A' Life, Simulant Synthetic

M Digital

B Concerned with the theme of genetic engineering and simulated post human life forms. For a personal book project 'Speculative Illustrations and Posthuman Photofictions'

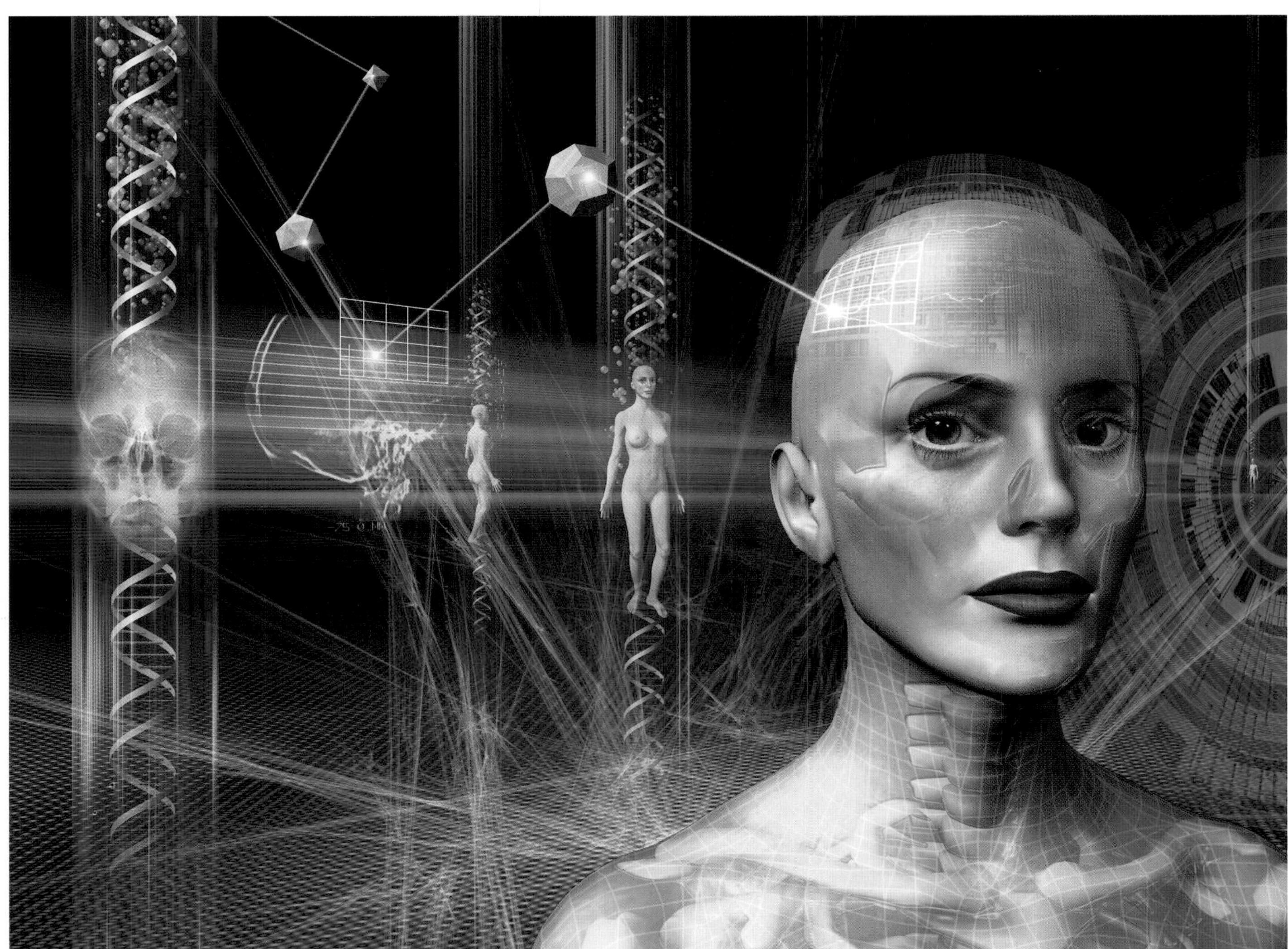

Martin Haake

Marie Claire

M Acrylic

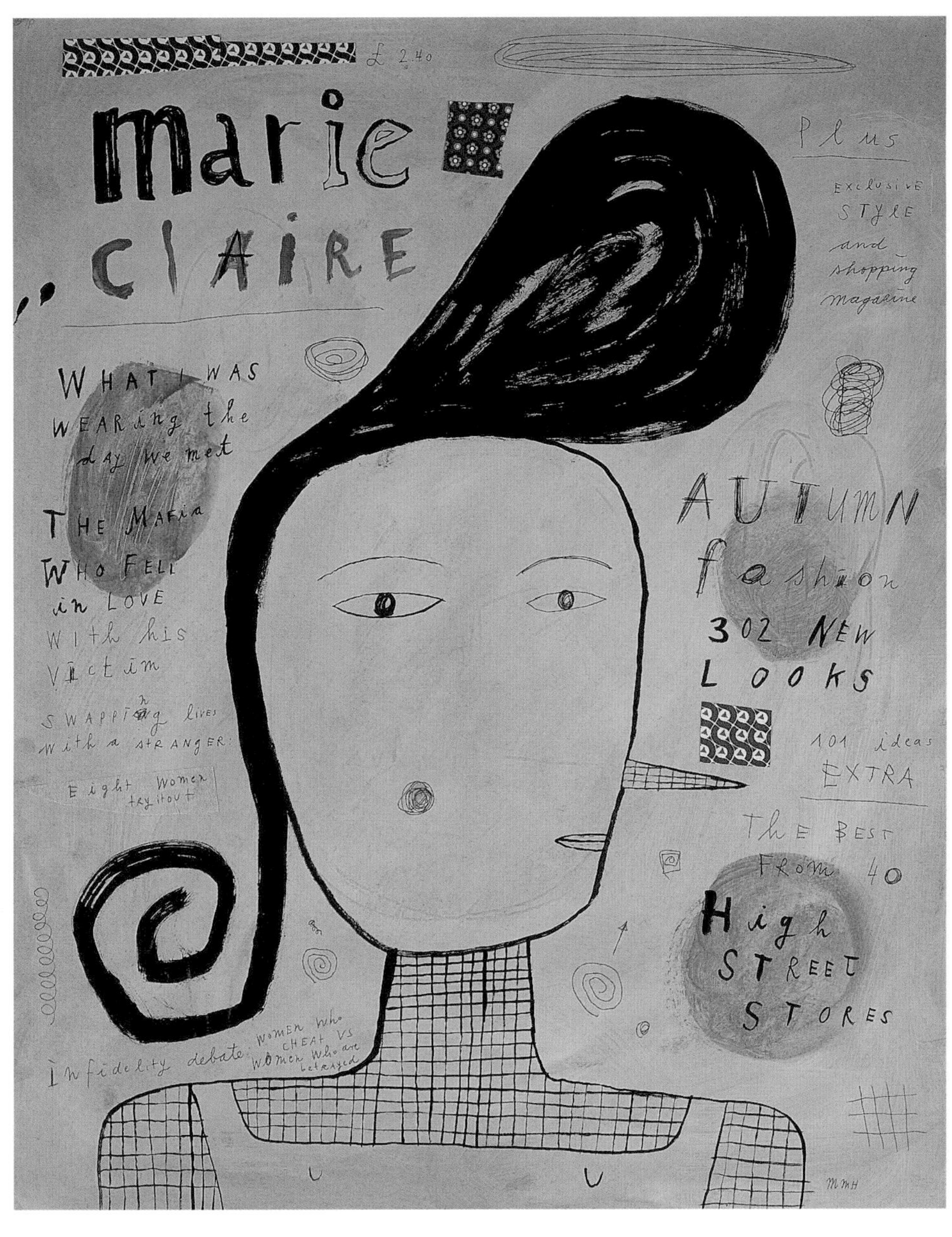

Andy Hammond
Hot Dog
M Pen, ink & watercolour
B Self promotional

Jo Hassall
Morris Minor
M Original art / digital
B Personal work, part of Domestic Bliss series

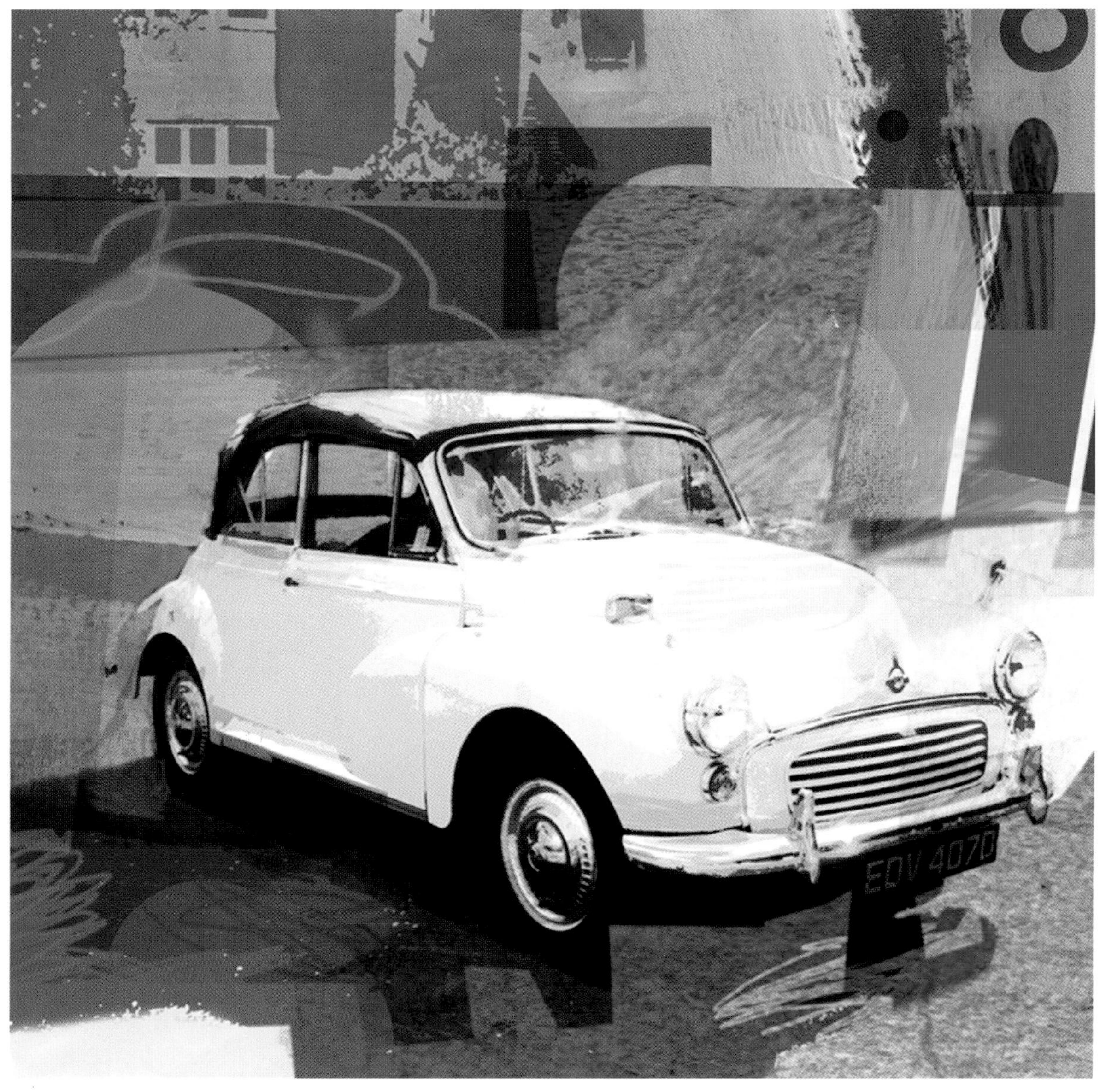

Kevin Hauff

S Access to All

M Mixed media

B Artwork that explores the difficulties for non–able bodied travellers trying to access more remote and adventurous destinations

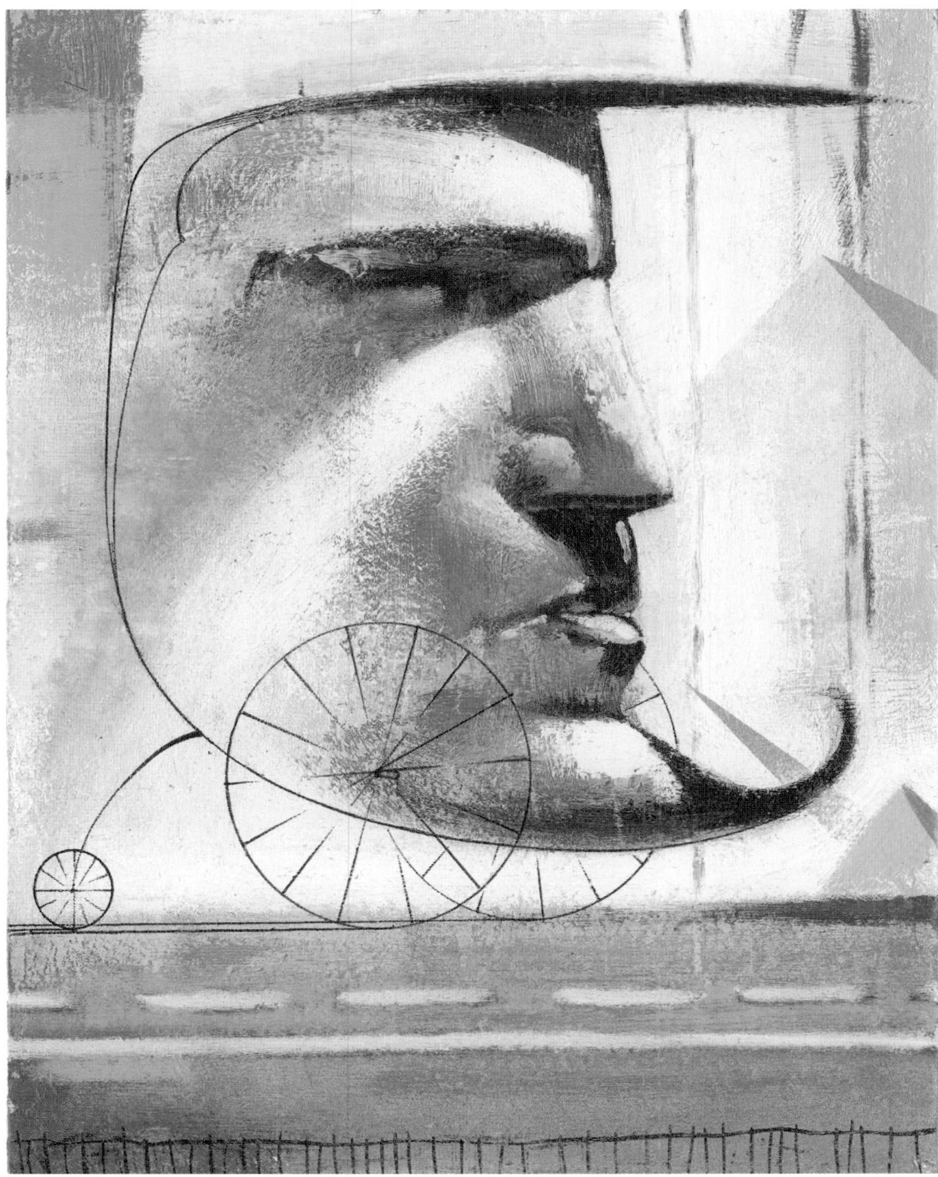

S

Kevin Hauff

Agoraphobic, Who, Me?

M Mixed media

B One of a series of images exploring one man's experience of suffering from and finally conquering acute agoraphobia, brought on by childhood trauma

Brownsite Optimism

M Mixed media

B Illustration exploring the recent positive change in attitudes relating to the strong potential in former derelict urban and industrial brown sites

Joanne Hayman
Bite

M Screenprint

B Produce a number of illustrations examining some of the curious attitudes of people towards their domestic pets

Robin Heighway-Bury
Famine

M Mixed media / digita

B Self initiated

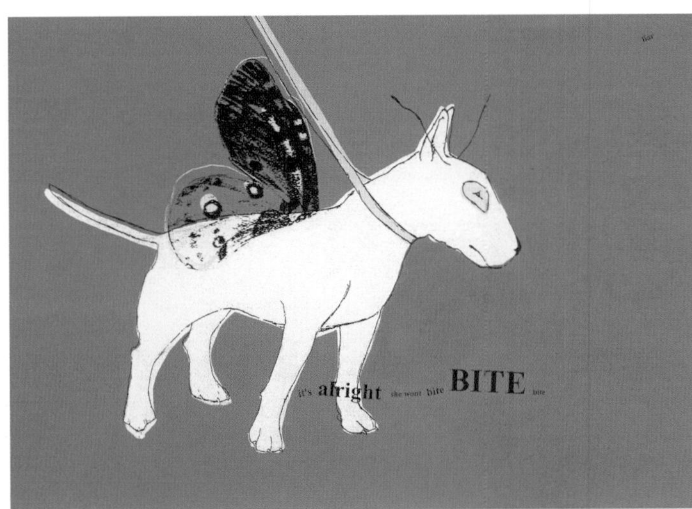

Marian Hill
Mr Punch

M Collage

B To illustrate Mr Punch, one of a set of four postage stamp designs on the theme of Punch and Judy produced for the Royal Mail

Grizelda Holderness
Rabbit

M Pastel

B Picture produced for exhibition – The Severnside Artists' Annual show

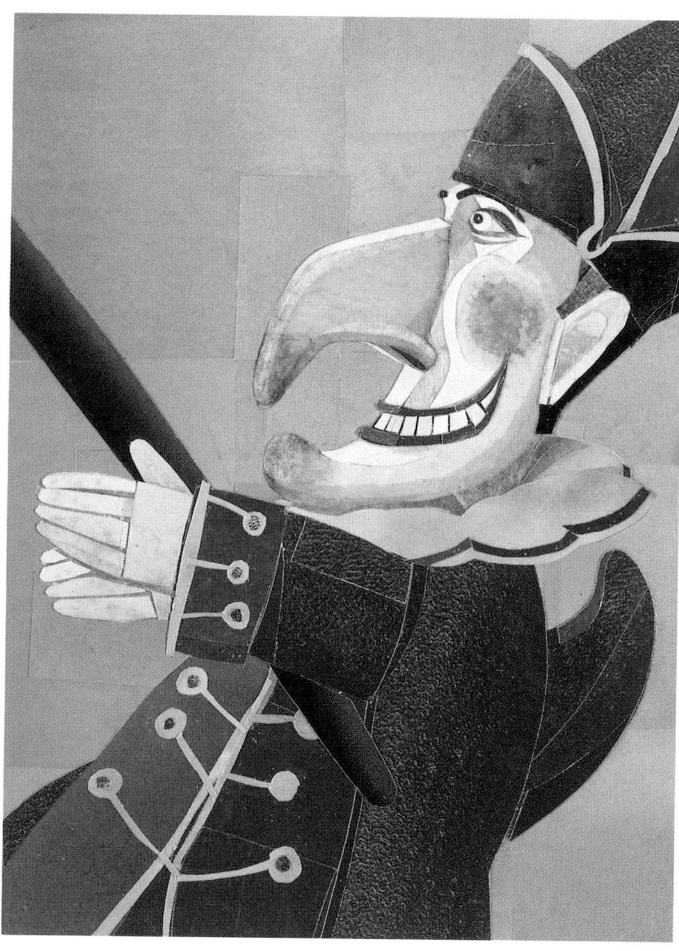

C Jane Ryan

F Royal Mail

Jasmine Hughes

B The Bluesman
M Collage, acrylic
B Self promotional / caricature

Who You Callin' Ugly?
M Collage, acrylic
B Self promotional / experimental project

B

Jasmine Hughes

Whips 'n' Chains

M Collage, acrylic

B One of a series of humorous images exploring alternative sexual lifestyles

Vinnie Jones

M Collage

B Self promotional / caricature

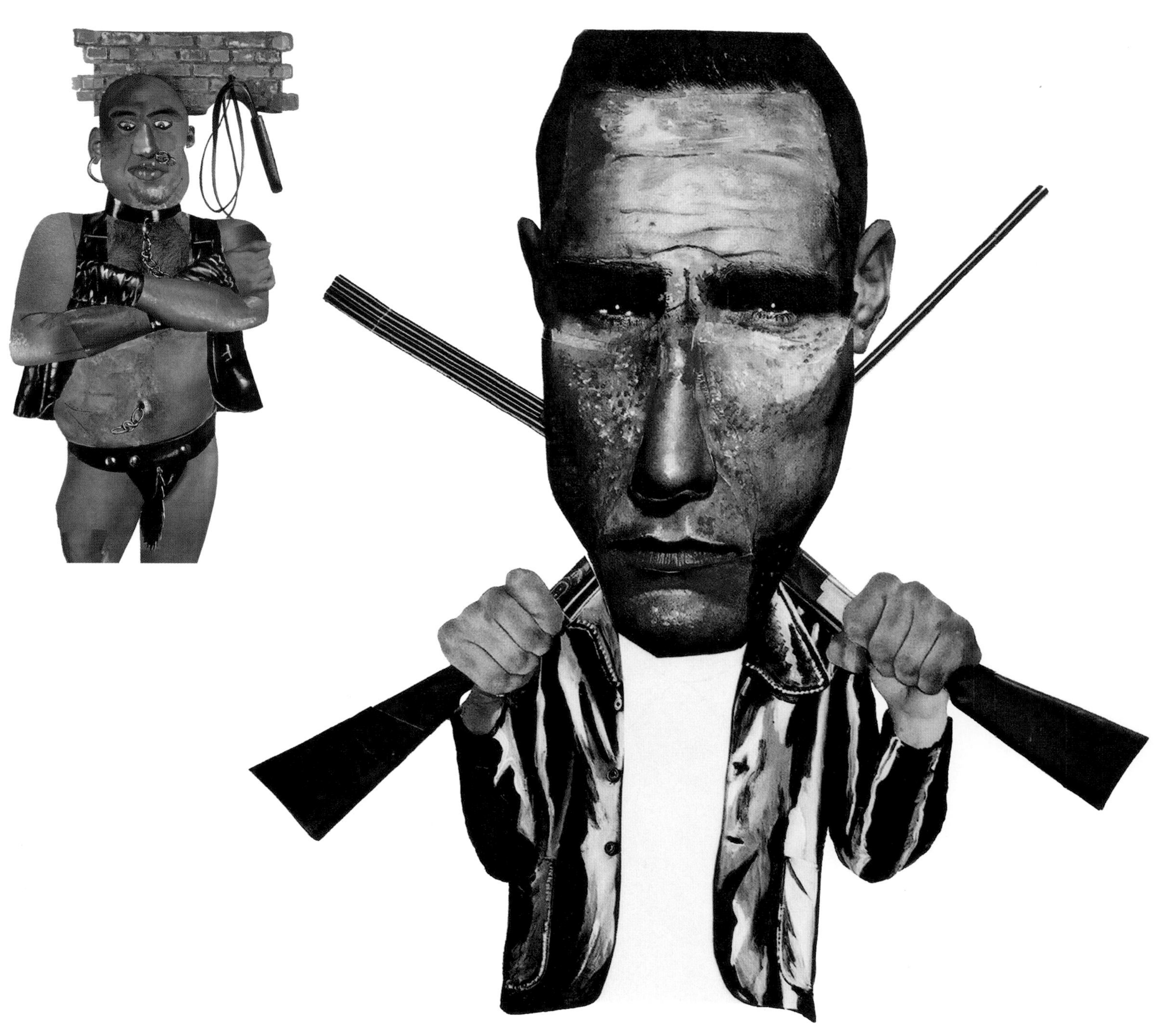

Stefan Isaacson
Daddy's Done Something Naughty

M Screenprint

B Editorial brief set by university: A mother's feelings on discovering that her husband had been interfering with their eight year old daughter

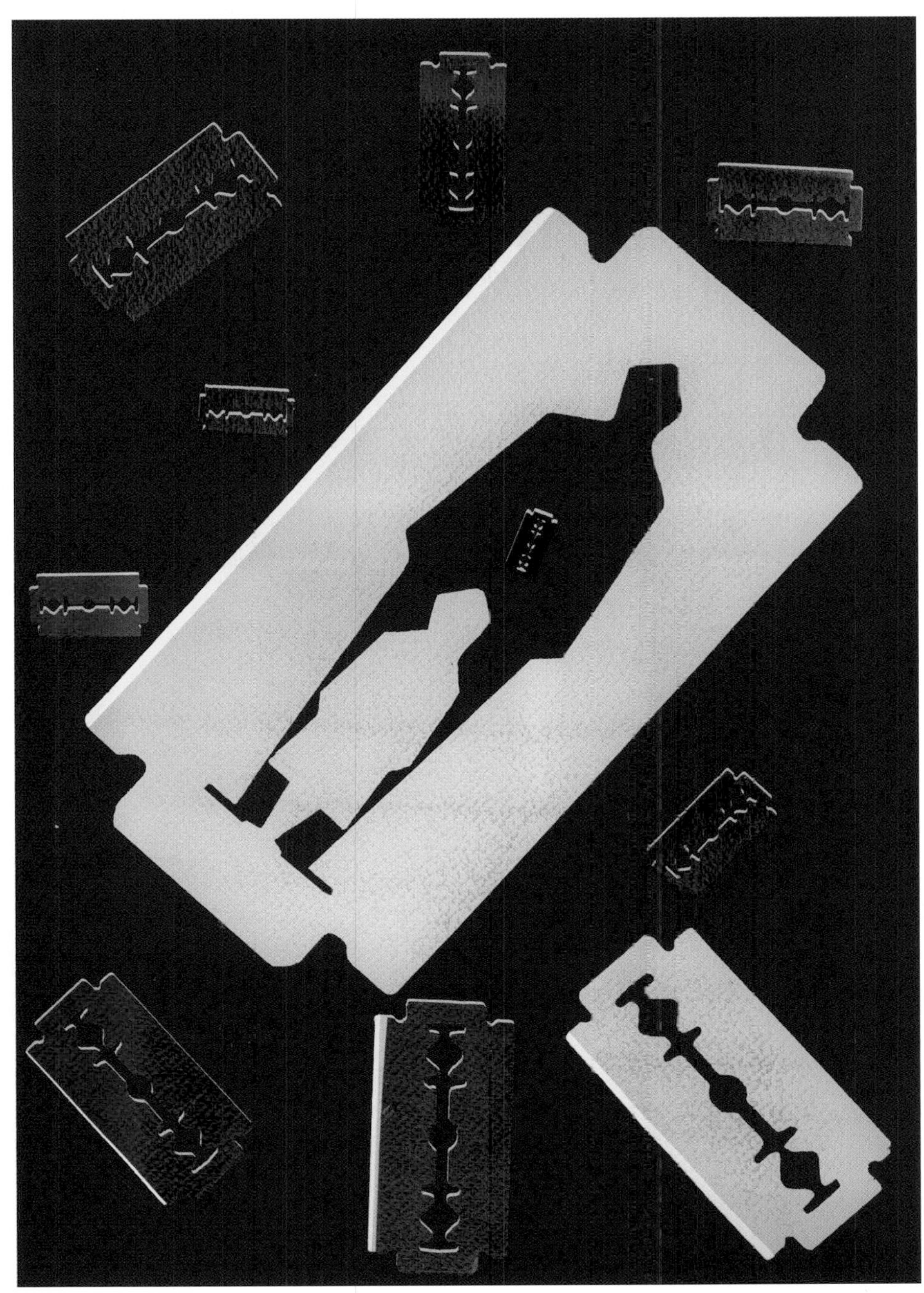

Satoshi Kambayashi
Beer Belly,
Hour Glass

M Digital

B Illustrate a couple with a contrasting degree of concern about their body.
Self promotional

Angela Lambert
Noah's Ark Playtray

M Acrylic, gouache (acrylgouache)

B Set of 4 board books for pre-school children within a playtray

Toby Leigh
Time Please
M Pen, ink, digital
B A portrayal of the ridiculous licensing laws in our country

Karin Littlewood
Sheep
M Pen and ink, gouache
B Personal piece

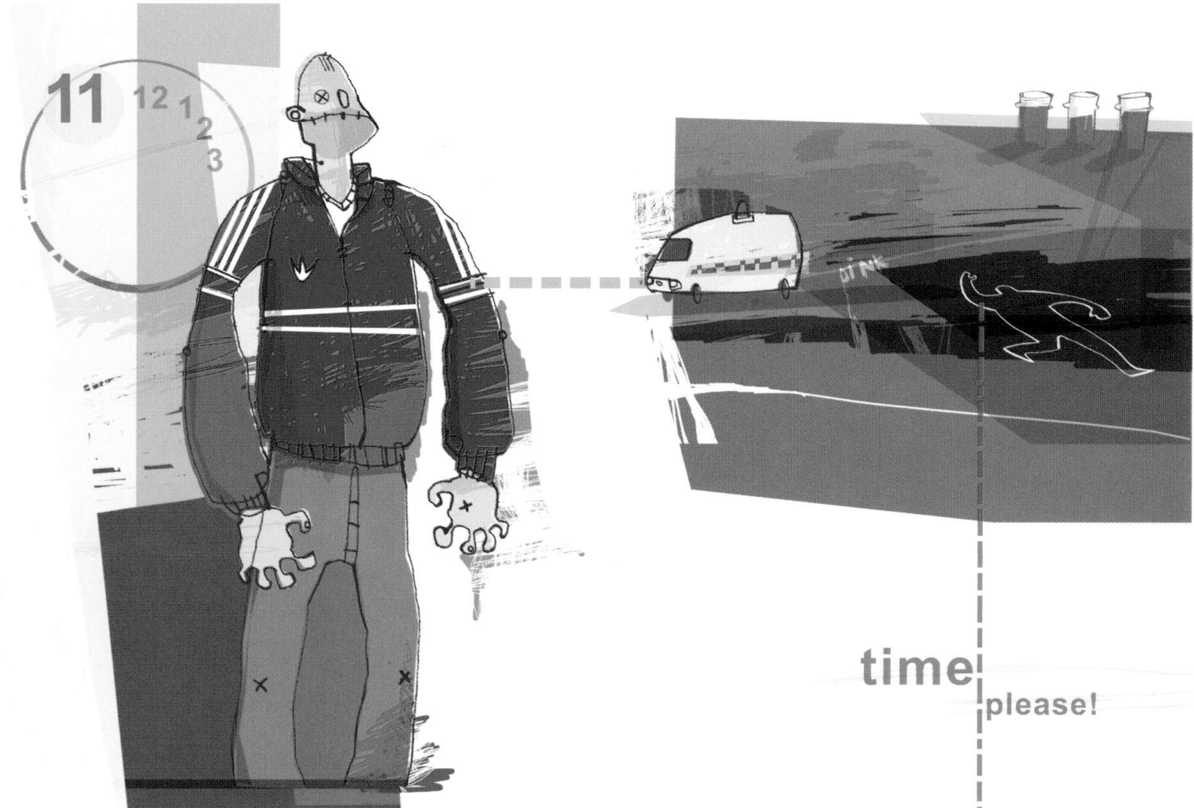

Oliver Lovley
Facelift

M Monoprint, collage

B Produce an image of one of the Seven Deadly Sins – Pride

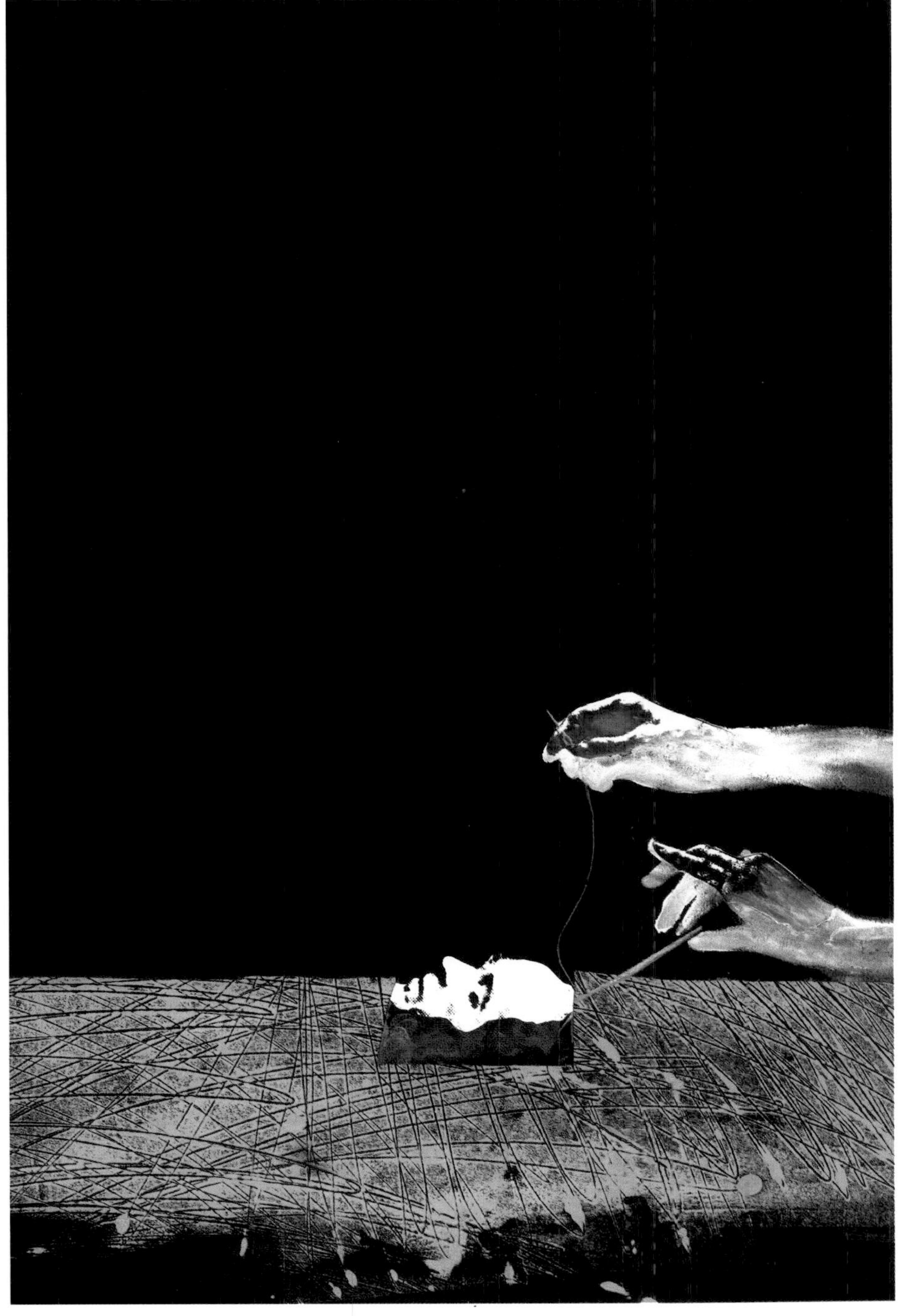

Katie Mac
Celeb
M Digital
B Self promotional

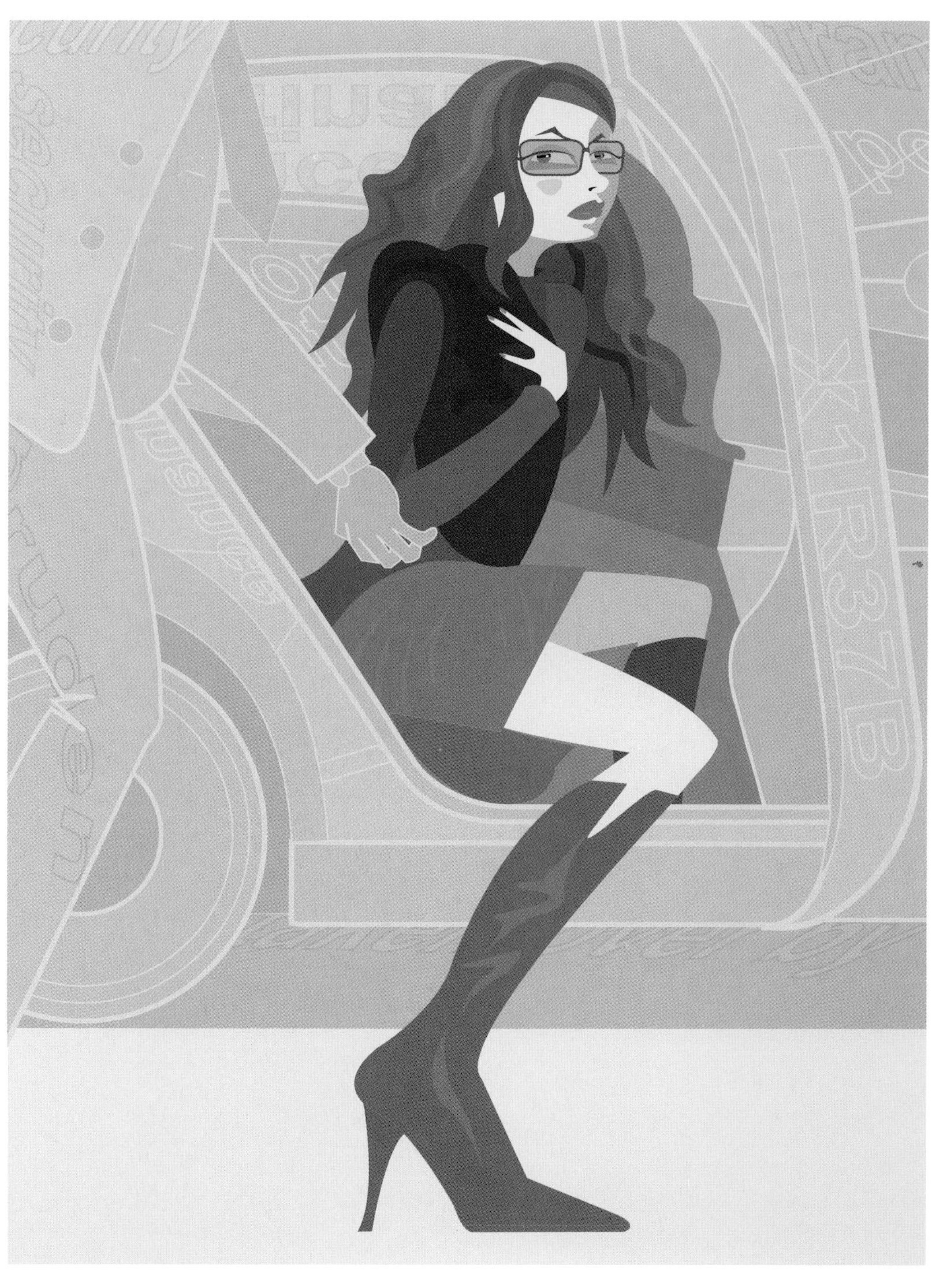

Mark Mackie
A Witness to the Fact
M Treated oil pastel
B An image in response to a text produced by the musicians called Wire

Tim Marrs

Firecracker

M Mixed media / digital

B Self promotional piece for own exhibition based on American car culture 'Start of Race'

Spirit of '56

M Mixed media / digital

B Self promotional piece for own exhibition based on American car culture 'End of Race'

James Marsh

The Environmentalist

M Acrylic on canvas

B Gallery and self promotional work

Michael Sheehy

Party Animal   Birthday Surprise

M Ink, watercolour

B Images for greetings cards – not used

Shin Shiraishi
B4 the Party
M Mixed media
B The girls images living in a city

Dionne Sievewright
Agapanthus
M Acrylic
B Produce an illustration representing the Island of Tresco, known as England's Island of Flowers. This particular Scillies Island is heavily influenced by the Mediterranean

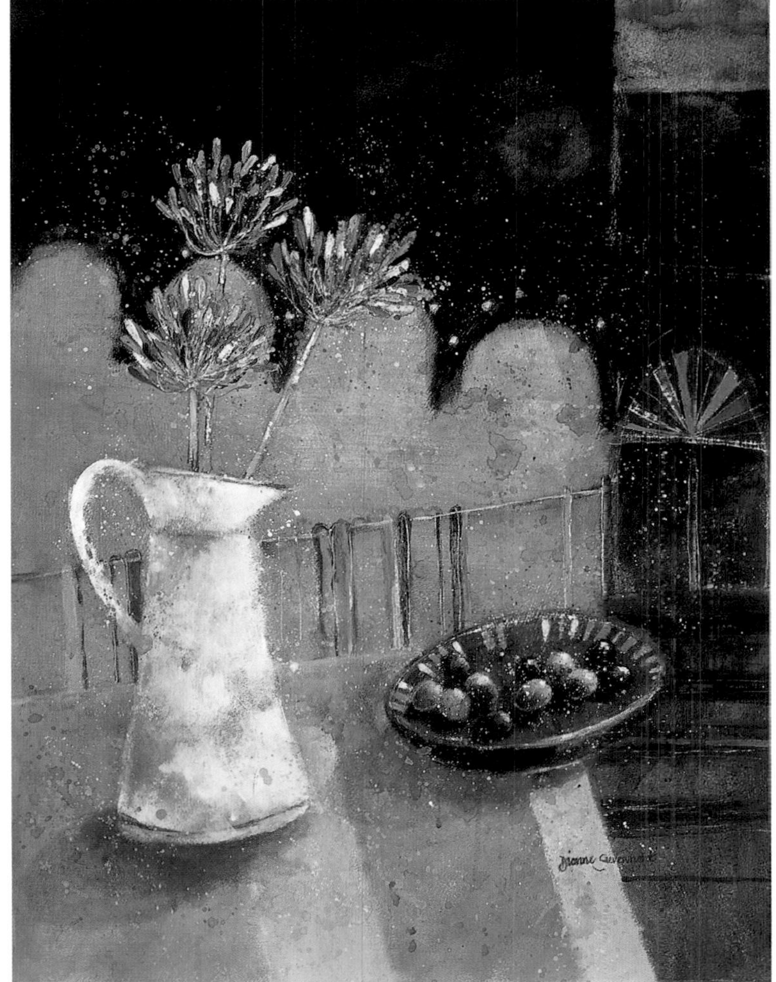

Lasse Skarbovik
Self-portrait
M Digital
B Self promotional work

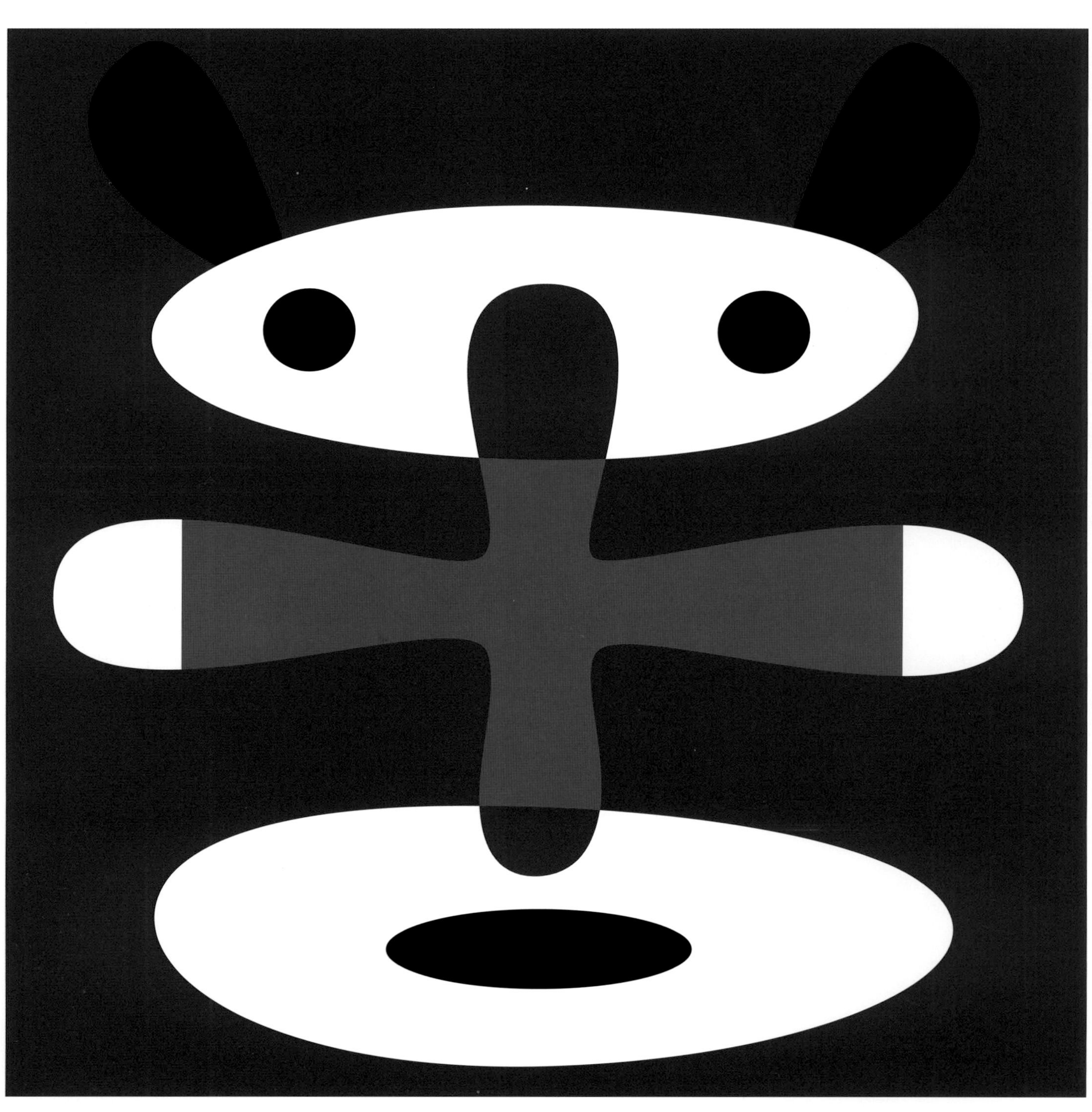

Simon Spilsbury

City Hell 1 City Hell 2

M Mixed media

B To represent claustrophobic city life

Karen Stannard
Chocolates
M Acrylic
B Self promotional

Tim Stevens
The Bazaar of Zanzib

M Pen, watercolour, gouache

B To give a sense of the hot, busy, colourful bazaar of Zanzib, our hero's home, alive with opportunity anything is for sale, even flying carpets...

Michelle Thompson

In a Free State

M Mixed media

B V.S. Naipaul's brilliantly written narrative history of scandals, betrayal, colonisation and forgotten lands

The Loss of El Dorado

M Mixed media

B V.S. Naipaul's haunting novel set in a free state in Africa, against a background of civil violence

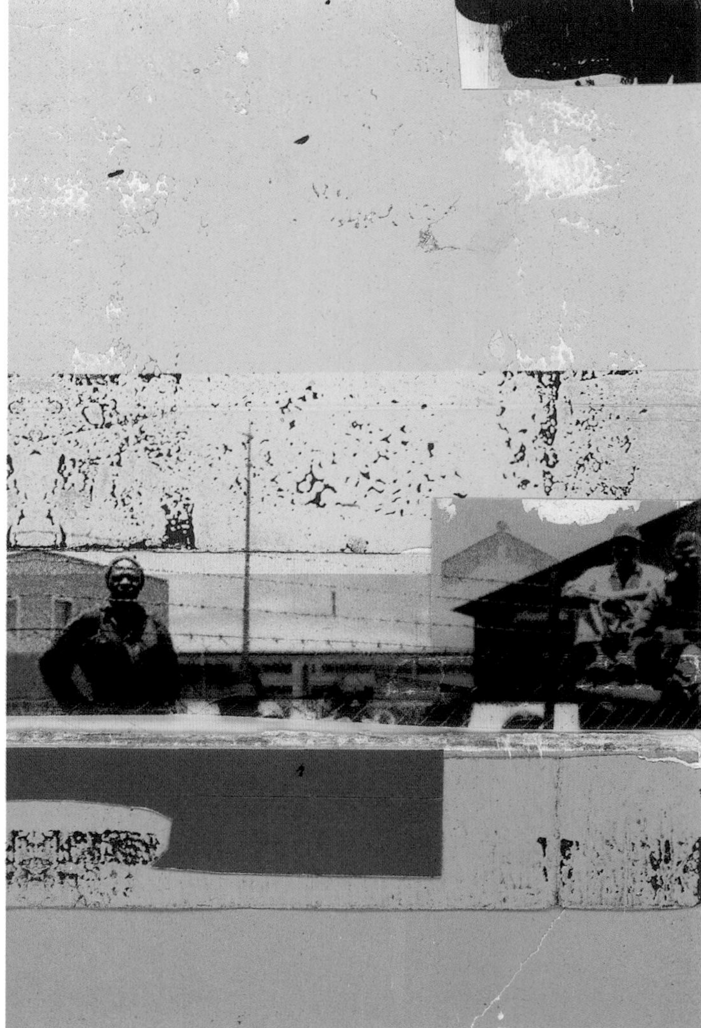

C Richard Evans

F Macmillan

C Richard Evans

F Macmillan

Mike Todd
Viagra
M Digital & mixed media
B Comment on the qualities of Viagra

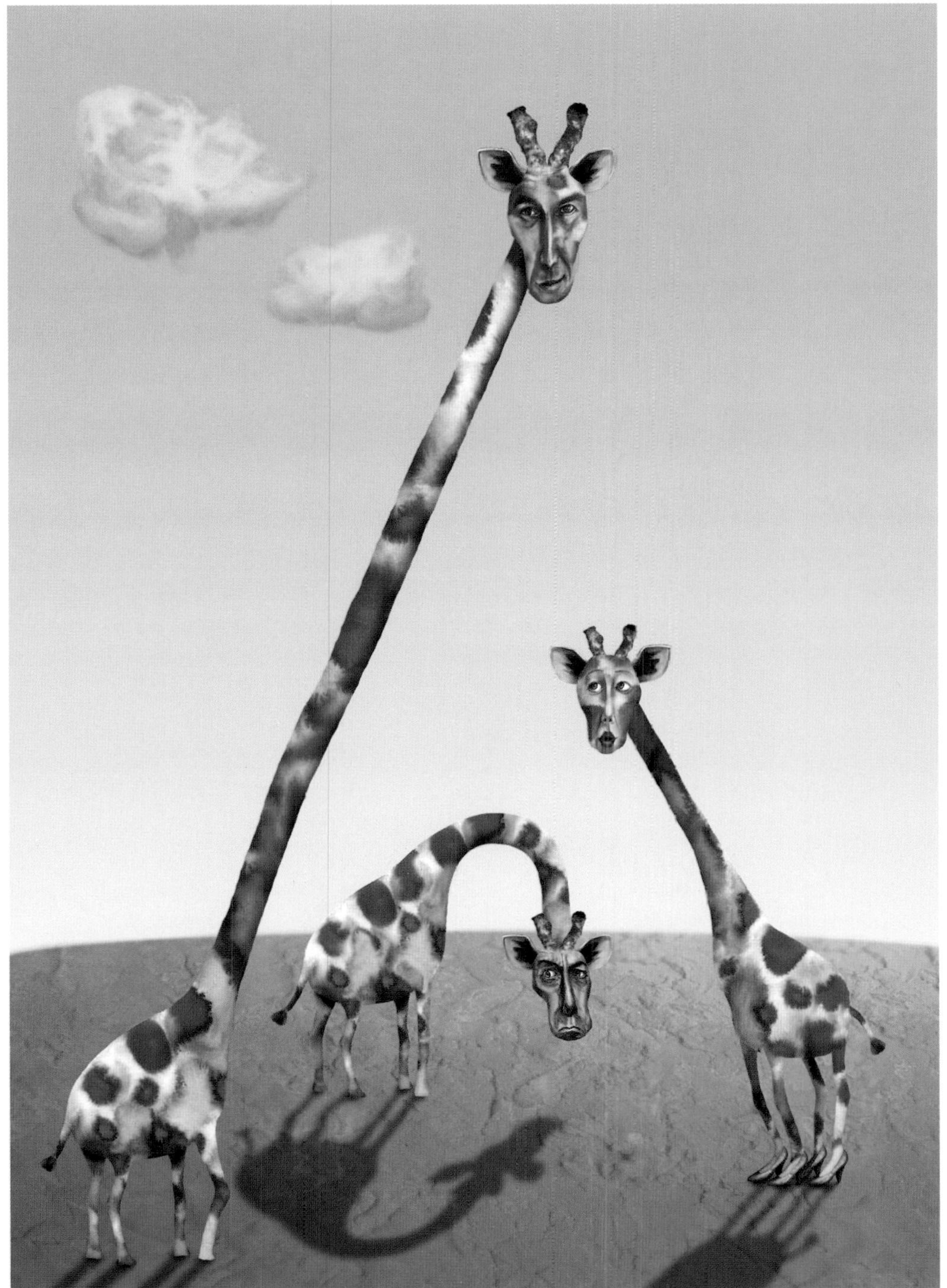

Jonathan Williams

Apology

M Digital

B You can tell that an apologetic person is sincere if they take responsibility for the error, instead of trying to shift the blame

Dr Foster

M Digital

B Dr Foster went to Gloucester
All in a shower of rain
He fell in a puddle
Right up to his middle...

Possibly Maybe

M Digital

B Electric shocks? She loves them!

Pat Garrett, Billy the Kid and the Cruel 44

M Digital

B Bob Dylan makes a cameo appearance in the film 'Pat Garrett and Billy the Kid'

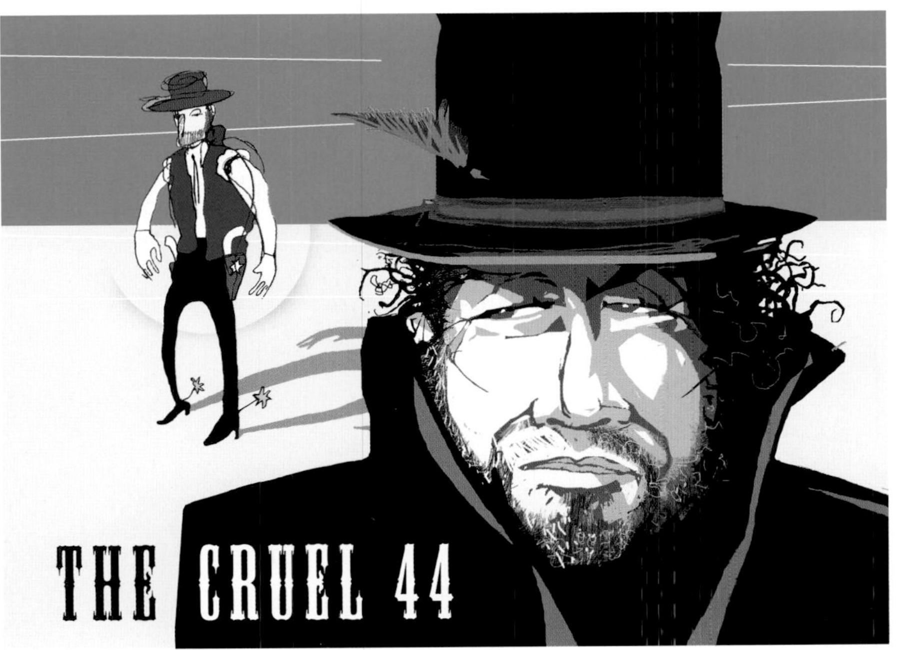

Lu Willis

'Say Cheese!'

M Gouache

B A young children's picture book about life as a twin, aimed at promoting positive images to black children in our multicultural society

They Unwrap the Presents, Sitting Back to Back

The First Day of School

Afiah
AbEn

Samantha Wilson
City Chic
M Mixed media
B To produce a set of mail outs directed towards fashion / lifestyle magazines

Adam Wilson
The Klompen Tree
M Pen and ink
B From a speculative publishing project 'The Klompen Tree'

AOI membership benefits

The Association of Illustrators provides a voice for professional illustrators and by force of numbers and expertise is able to enforce the rights of freelance illustrators at every stage of their careers. Membership of the AOI is open to all illustrators, illustration students, agents, lecturers and illustration clients.

All categories of membership receive the following benefits:
- Bi-monthly journal
- Discounted rate for Images – entry fees, publication rates and hanging fees
- Contact details on office database for enquiries from clients
- Discounts from material suppliers
- Regional group contacts
- Discounts on AOI events and publications

In addition we provide the following services for particular types of membership:

Full Membership
This category is for professional illustrators who have had work commissioned and accept the AOI code of conduct:
- Legal advice on contracts
- Hotline information on pricing and professional practice
- Discounted portfolio surgery
- Business advice – an hour's free consultation with a chartered accountant on accounts, book-keeping, National Insurance, VAT and tax
- Full members are entitled to use the affix 'Mem AOI'
- Discounts on AOI events and publications

Associate Membership
This one-year category is for newcomers and illustrators in their first year out of college who have not published work. In exceptional circumstances this membership can be extended by an extra year:
- Hotline information on pricing and professional practice
- Discounted portfolio surgery
- Business advice – an hour's free consultation with a chartered accountant on accounts, book-keeping, National Insurance, VAT and tax

Student Membership
This service is for students on full-time illustration or related courses:
- See above services for all AOI members
- Discounted portfolio surgery

Corporate Membership
This service is agents and clients from the illustration industry:
- Bi-monthly journal
- Free copy of the Images catalogue
- All corporate members' staff and illustrators will receive discounts on events, Images and AOI publications

For an application form and cost details please contact:
Association of Illustrators
81 Leonard Street
London EC2A 4QS
T +44 (0)20 7613 4328
F +44 (0)20 7613 4417
E info@a-o-illustrators.demon.co.uk
W www.aoi.co.uk
www.aoisupplement.co.uk

College Membership
College membership entitles the college to the following benefits:
- A free lecture from an AOI Council Member or selected illustrator on the creative, ethical and business aspects of illustration
- Free copy of Images annual
- AOI bi-monthly journal

AOI publications

Survive: The Illustrators Guide to a Professional Career
Published by the AOI, Survive is the only comprehensive and in-depth guide to illustration as a professional career. Established illustrators, agents, clients and a range of other professionals have contributed to this edition. Each area of the profession including portfolio presentation, self promotion and copyright issues are looked at in detail. The wealth of information in Survive makes it absolutely indispensable to the newcomer and also has much to offer the more experienced illustrator.

Rights: The Illustrators Guide to Professional Practice
Rights is an all inclusive guide to aspects of the law specifically related to illustration. It includes information about copyright, contracts, book publishing agreements, agency agreements, how to go about seeking legal advice, how to calculate fees and guidance on how to write a licence.

Rights is the result of a number of years research. It has been approved by solicitors and contains the most detailed and accurate model terms and conditions available for use by illustrators or clients.

Troubleshooting Guide
A handbook written by solicitors Ruth Gladwin and Robert Lands (Finers Stephens Innocent) covering essential legal issues surrounding subjects such as animation, collage, websites, and advice about taking cases to the small claims court.

Client Directories
Both Publishing and Editorial Directories list over 100 illustration clients with full contact details: the Advertising Directory holds details of over 200 advertising agencies who commission illustration – providing an invaluable source of information for all practitioners.

www.aoi.co.uk

Portfolios

A huge range of illustrators' portfolios, from both member and non-members. Regularly updated, the Gallery now contains hundreds of images that are easily searchable by artist's name or subject. Images are initially viewed as thumbnails with the artist's name providing a link to their contact details and biography. Its never been simpler to find the illustrator you've been searching for.

News

Up to date industry news is regularly recorded. News archives are searchable by year, month and keyword.

Magazine

The Association's monthly magazine on-line. Archives contain a wealth of material fully searchable by keyword.

Forum

The place to post your thoughts and enter discussion on any topics of concern to the illustration community.

Info

General information about the AOI including a full list of services, events, publications and membership.

Publications

Gives details of all the AOI publications, including Images. The AOI publishes an invaluable series of guides for illustrators, each one packed with authoritative information: Survive, Rights and the Troubleshooting Guide, the handbook for legal issues affecting illustrators. Details are listed under Essentials. Also available are the excellent directories for Editorial, Publishing and Advertising.

Other Features

Personal Web Address

Illustrators appearing on the site can have a personal web address linked directly to their images.

Postcards

Any chosen image from the Gallery can be mailed together with a message as an electronic 'postcard'. Illustrators or agents wishing to submit images to the Gallery can find complete details on-line or by telephoning the AOI office. AOI on-line has been developed for the Association of Illustrators by Warp Interactive.

www.aoisupplement.co.uk

The AOI's Supplement page primarily serves as an online archive of the history of the Association. Very much a work in progress, publications, books, magazines and ephemera are all being digitised and added to the site. Additionally the site showcases special AOI events such as auctions and book premieres and also provides comprehensive links to other illustration-related material on the web.

- **Online Directory**
  Live links with thumbnails to illustrators' homepages. Full listings for agents (both here and abroad), other illustration associations, colleges and general resources.
- **Images History**
  Who appeared in each annual and who judged that year. Full listings.
- **Journal History**
  Dating back to the first issue in 1974 the covers index lists the contents for each issue and provides links to available online texts.
- **Images 25**
  The complete book.
- **Downloads**
  Membership/entry/booking forms are all available here for download in pdf format. Also includes back issues of the Despatch newsletter.

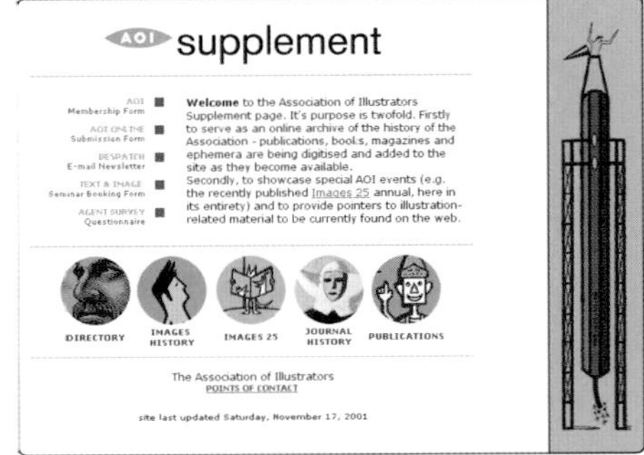

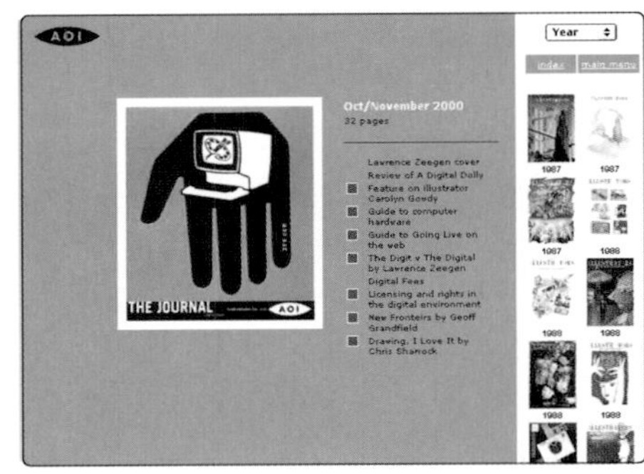

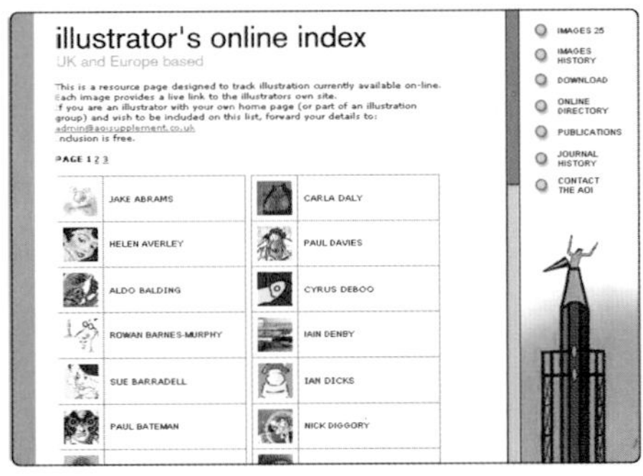

The essential illustration magazine

The AOI Journal, re-launched in Summer 2000, covers a wide range of issues related to the illustration industry including:

- current industry affairs
- illustration events
- reviews
- interviews
- letters

Regular contributors include educators, practitioners and industry professionals. The Journal provides a forum for on-going debate, and a valuable insight into contemporary illustration.

Published six times a year, the Journal is free to members. To subscribe to the AOI Journal as a non-member, please send a cheque for £30, made payable to the Association of Illustrators, to:

Journal Subscription
Association of Illustrators
81 Leonard Street
London EC2A 4QS

For payment by Visa, Mastercard or Switch please call **T** 020 7613 4328

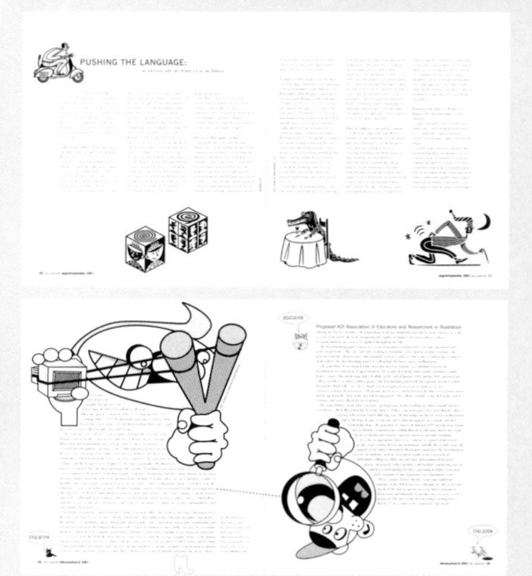

Grizelda Holderness 216
Parks Cottage
The Green
Frampton-on-Severn
Gloucestershire GL2 7DU
T 01452 740 359
A Illustration Ltd
1 Vicarage Crescent
London SW11 3LP
T 020 7228 8882
E team@illustrationweb.com
W www.mywholeportfolio.com/GrizeldaHolderness

Gina Holley 163
71 Norbiton Hall
Birkenhead Avenue
Kingston upon Thames
Surrey KT2 6RR
T 020 8974 8158
M 07899 046 670
E gina.holley@btopenworld.com

David Holmes 150
5 Calvert Street
Primrose Hill
London NW1 8NE
T 020 7586 0363
F 020 7586 8907
M 07976 872 377
E david@cecilholmes.demon.co.uk
A Central Illustation Agency
36 Wellington Street
London WC2E 7BD
T 020 7836 1106
W www.centralillustration.com

Peter Horridge 38
Maribonne
Bunbury Lane
Bunbury
Tarporley
Cheshire CW6 9QS
T 01829 261 801
F 01829 261 801
M 07775 583 760
E peter@horridge.com
W www.horridge.com

Anne Howeson 77
91 Cloudesley Road
London N1 0EL
T 020 7837 2939
F 020 7837 2939
E aehoweson@aol.com

Suzanna Hubbard 151
24 St George's Road
Brighton
East Sussex BN2 1ED
T 01273 681 076
F 01273 681 076
M 07939 025 003
E zanna.hubbard@virgin.net
A The Organisation
Basement
69 Caledonian Road
London N1 9BT
T 020 7833 8268
E organise@easynet.co.uk
W www.organisart.co.uk

Frazer Hudson 77
M 07973 616 054
E frazer@dircon.co.uk
W www.frazer.dircon.co.uk

Mark Hudson 151
20A Cloudsley Square
London N1 0HN
T 020 7253 2807
F 020 7253 2807
M 07050 128 125
E m.hudson.esq@virgin.net

Jasmine Hughes 217-218
21 Frondeg
Llandegfan
Anglesey LL59 5TN
T 01248 713 402
E khugbear@aol.com

Ruth Hulbert 164
21 Exning Road
Canning Town
London E16 4NB
T 020 7473 4517
M 07870 416 528
E rehulbert@hotmail.com

Rebecca Husbands 165
49 The Ferns
Larkfield
Aylesford
Kent ME20 6NF
T 01732 840 138
M 07769 585 530
E beckhusbands@hotmail.com

Stefan Isaacson 219
17 Englefield Drive
Oakenholt
Flint
Flintshire CH6 5SB
M 07719 940 265
E stefanisaacson@hotmail.com
W www.stefanisaacson.freeservers.com

Katy Jackson 166
Trees
St Nicholas Avenue
Great Bookham
Surrey KT23 4AY
T 01372 452 901
M 07816 171 881
E katy_jackson80@hotmail.com
W www.wow-illustration.co.uk

Benoit Jacques 78
32 rue Raymont Frot
F-77690 Montigny-sur-Loing
France
T +33 1 64 45 62 94
F +33 1 64 45 63 10

Adrian Johnson 130
A Arena
108 Leonard Street
London EC2A 4RH
T 020 7613 4040
E info@arenaworks.com
W www.arenaworks.com

Matthew Johnson 80
355, Clerkenwell Workshops
31 Clerkenwell Close
London EC1R 0AT
T 020 7336 7832
M 07941 516 449

Richard Johnson 79, 131
41 Highcroft Avenue
Oadby
Leicester LE2 5UH
T 0116 271 9380
M 07931 136 235
E rich@richj84.freeserve.co.uk
W www.thesmallpicture.co.uk

Akiko Kamae 167
04-12-07 Shioya-Kitamachi
Tarumi-ku
Kobe, Hyogo
Japan 655 0863
T +81 78 753 6370
F +81 78 753 6370
E kamae@zc5.so-net.ne.jp
W www18.u-page.so-net.ne.jp/zc5/kamae/

Satoshi Kambayashi 81, 220
Flat 2
40 Tisbury Road
Hove
East Sussex BN3 3BA
T 01273 771 539
F 01273 771 539
P 07626 131 519
E satoshi.k@virgin.net
W www.satoshi-illustration.com

Chris Kasch 82
27 Butler Road
West Harrow
Middlesex HA1 4DS
T 020 8422 2416

Angela Lambert 221
Vine Cottage
South Street
Avebury Trusloe
Wiltshire SN8 1QX
T 01672 539 322
F 01672 539 352
M 07801 480 241
E angel@thumbnail.demon.co.uk
W www.thumbnail.demon.co.uk

Matt Lee 168
11 Blaney Way
Corfe Mullen
Wimborne
Dorset BH21 3UG
T 01202 699 689
M 07759 984 669
E mattlee1000@hotmail.com

Sean Lee 82
72 Promenade
Portabello
Edinburgh EH15 2DX
T 01316 574 369

Toby Leigh 222
59 Elmar Road
London N15 5DH
M 07976 939 853
E tobatron@hotmail.com

Karin Littlewood 130, 222
Courtyard Studio
38 Mount Pleasant
London WC1X 0AP
T 020 7833 4113
F 020 7833 3064
M 07941 651 806

Henning Löhlein 83
CentreSpace
6 Leonard Lane
Bristol BS1 1EA
T 0117 929 9077
F 0117 929 9077
M 07711 285 202
E lohlein@aol.com
W www.lohlein.com

Oliver Lovley 223
13 Highbury Road
Keyworth
Nottinghamshire NG12 5JB
T 0115 846 1814
M 07949 835 441
E oliver.lovley@ntlworld.com

Richard Lyon 168
10 Greenland Close
North Anston
Sheffield S25 4AW
T 01909 562 544
M 07979 935 559
E richard_lyon70@hotmail.com
W www.geocities.com/rlyonuk/ills

Katie Mac 224
4a Kimmerston House
1 Udall Street
SW1P 2PR
T 07812 120 342
M 07968 101 606
E katiemac91@hotmail.com
W www.katiemac.co.uk

Patrick MacAllister 132
23 Vicars Oak Road
London SE19 1HE
T 020 8761 5578
F 020 8761 5578
E patrick.hat@talk21.com

Mark Mackie 225
Hill View
Cornhill
Hemyock
Devon EX15 3RQ
T 01823 680 733
E mark.mackie@btopenworld.com

Tim Marrs 226
33B Waldegrave Road
Upper Norwood
London SE19 2AL
T 020 8653 8044
M 07714 062 447
E tim.marrs@virgin.net
W www.timmarrs.co.uk
A Central Illustration Agency
36 Wellington Street
London WC2E 7BD
T 020 7240 8925
W www.centralillustration.com

James Marsh
84, 85, 132, 227
21 Elms Road
London SW4 9ER
T 020 7622 9530
F 020 7498 6851
E james@james-marsh.co.uk
W www.jamesmarsh.com

Mick Marston 39
6 Holtwood Road
Sheffield S4 7BA
T 0114 281 8440
M 07799 487 795
E mikiluv@blueyonder.co.uk
W www.mikiluv.com

Steve May 20, 40
A Arena
108 Leonard Street
London EC2A 4RH
T 020 7613 4040
E info@arenaworks.com
W www.arenaworks.com

Debra McFarlane 152
33 Elmbridge Avenue
Tolworth
Surbiton
Surrey KT5 9EZ
T 020 8390 0627
M 07979 937 281

Alan McGowan 88
3 Montgomery Street
Edinburgh EH7 5JU
T 0131 557 2396
M 07980 845 629
E mail@alanmcgowan.com
W www.illustrationart.net

Shane Mc Gowan 86-87
23A Parkholme Road
London E8 3AG
T 020 7249 6444
A Three in a Box
468 Queen Street East
Suite 104, Box 03
Toronto (ON), Canada
M5A 1T7
T 020 8853 1236

Mark McLaughlin 228
Clockwork Studios
38a Southwell Road
London SE5 9PG
T/F 020 7924 0921
T/F 020 8761 7946 (home)
E markmcl10@aol.com
W www.contact-me.net/MarkMcLaughlin
www.portfolios.com/MarkMclaughlin

Amy McSimpson 169
Brook House
Old School Lane
Brockham
Surrey RH3 7JP
T 01737 843 235
M 07789 503 456
E amymc79@hotmail.com

Tony Meeuwissen 41
2 Cromer Cottages
Stroud
Gloucestershire GL5 5DQ
T 01453 873 135

Belle Mellor 89-91
Flat 3
12 Lansdowne Street
Hove
East Sussex BN3 1FQ
T 01273 732 604
F 01273 732 604
M 07973 463 942
E belle.mellor@virgin.net
A Three in a Box
468 Queen Street East
Suite 104, Box 03
Toronto (ON), Canada
M5A 1T7
T +1 416 367 2446

Samantha Meredith 170
37 Park Road
Cosby
Leicester LE9 1RN
M 07779 089 039
E smooantha@
hotmail.com

José Luis Merino 92
A Kate Larkworthy
Artist Representation Ltd
16 Rickbern Street
NY-10580 Rye USA
T +1 914 925 9672
F +1 914 925 0370
W www.larkworthy.com

Adria Meserve 133
91 Vartry Road
South Tottenham
London N15 6QD
T 020 8880 1834
M 07944 501 352
E adriameserve@
elmsi.freeserve.co.uk

Jessica Mikhail 171
352 Hay Green Lane
Bournville
Birmingham B30 1SR
T 0121 475 7518

Kate Miller 93
M 07958 998 078
E kate@
hannayk.freeserve.co.uk
A Central Illustration Agency
36 Wellington Street
London WC2E 7BD
T 020 7240 8925
W www.
centralillustration.com

Gunnlaug Moen Hembery 42, 93
30 Rodway Road
Patchway
Bristol
South Gloucestershire
BS34 5PJ
T 0117 969 7995
M 07748 792 493
E Gunnlaug.Moen@
btinternet.com
W www.gunnlaug.co.uk

Julie Monks 43
521 Clerkenwell Workshops
31 Clerkenwell Close
London EC1R 0AT
T 020 7490 4872
F 020 7490 4872
M 07930 347 016
A Peters, Fraser & Dunlop
Drury House
34-43 Russell Street
London WC2B 5HA
T 020 7344 1000

Lydia Monks 21, 134
Courtyard Studio
38 Mount Pleasant
London WC1X 0AP
T 020 7833 4113
F 020 7833 3064
M 07971 052 529
A Hilary Delamere
The Agency
24 Pottery Lane
Holland Park
London W11 4LZ
T 020 7727 1346

Amanda Montgomery-Higham 228
Tregonna
Church Street
Carharrack
Redruth
Cornwall TR16 5RW
T 01209 820 555
M 07960 892 669
E Amanda@montgomery-
higham.fsnet.co.uk

David 'Martin' Morrison 229
20 Fredora Avenue
Hayes
Middlesex UB4 8RB
T/F 020 8797 2632
M 07980 028 235
E d4martin@hotmail.com

Sheila Moxley 135
138 Glenarm Road
Clapton
London E5 0NB
T 020 7490 4872
020 8533 3583
F 020 7490 4872
M 07905 770 398
E sheila@sheilamoxley.com
W www.sheilamoxley.com
www.contact-me.net/
SheilaMoxley

Ian Murray 44, 94-95
A Illustration Ltd
1 Vicarage Crescent
London SW11 3LP
T 020 7228 8882
E team@
illustrationweb.com
W www.mywholeportfolio.
com/IanMurray

Sarah Nayler 44
A NB Illustration
40 Bowling Green Lane
London EC1R 0NE
T 020 7278 9131
W www.nbillustration.co.uk

Gary Neill 230
17A Romberg Road
Tooting Bec
London SW17 8UB
M 07973 866 739
A Central Illustration Agency
36 Wellington Street
London WC2E 7BD
T 020 7240 8925
W www.
centralillustration.com

Ray Nicklin 21, 230
26 Alma Road
Cardiff CF23 5BD
T 029 2049 3432
F 029 2049 3432
E raynicklin@aol.com
rnicklin@uwic.ac.uk

Arnie Nisbet 96
37B Corinne Road
London N19 5EZ
T 020 7607 3652
M 07808 739 604
E an@arnienisbet.com
W www.arnienisbet.com
A Illustration Ltd
1 Vicarage Crescent
London SW11 3LP
T 020 7228 8882
E team@
illustrationweb.com

Tilly Northedge 45, 46
Grundy & Northedge
Power Road Studios
114 Power Road
London W4 5PY
T 020 8995 2452
E tilly@
grundynorthedge.com
W www.
grundynorthedge.com

Kevin O'Keefe 97, 23[illegible]
38 Osborne Road
Bristol BS3 1PW
T 0117 963 3835
F 0117 963 3835
M 07740 942 382
E jokevanoke@
blueyonder.co.uk
A Art Box Amsterdam
T +31 (0) 20 668 1551
F +31 (0) 20 693 9907
E info@artbox.nl
W www.artbox.nl

Martin O'Neill 98
Studio 18, Cornwell House
21 Clerkenwell Green
London EC1R 0DP
T 020 7251 0071
F 020 7251 0071
M 07931 533 041

Mel Owen 232
2 Garden Cottages
Lydhurst
Warninglid
West Sussex RH17 5TG
T 01444 461 996
M 07939 037 239
E mellyowen@hotmail.com
W http://homepage.mac.
com/illustrate

Nigel Owen 98
1 Estuary View
Beacon Street
Falmouth
Cornwall TR11 2AQ
T 01326 211 053
F 01326 211 053
M 07941 797 363
E nigelowen@
macunlimited.net
A Central Illustration Agency
36 Wellington Street
London WC2E 7BD
T 020 7240 8925
W www.
centralillustration.com

Paquebot 99, 233, 234
Flat 2
40 Tisbury Road
Hove
East Sussex BN3 3BA
T 01273 771 539
F 01273 771 539
E le paquebot@virgin.net
W www.
satoshi-illustration.com

Antony Parnell 235
55 Portia Way
Mile End
London E3 4JG
M 07979 916 499
E antony.d.parnell@
talk21.com
A Début Art
30 Tottenham Street
London W1 9PN
T 020 7636 1064
W www.debutart.com

Garry Parsons
99, 136, 237
249 Bellenden Road
London SE15 4DQ
T 020 7358 1856
020 7490 1882
M 07931 923 934
E bachimitsu@aol.com
A Meiklejohn Illustration
5 Risborough Street
London SE1 0HF
T 020 7593 0500
W www.meiklejohn.co.uk

Jackie Parsons 236
3rd Floor Studio
5 Torrens Street
London EC1V 5NQ
T 020 7837 4629
F 020 7837 4629
M 07957 121 818
E parsons@dircon.co.uk
A Central Illustration Agency
36 Wellington Street
London WC2E 7BD
T 020 7240 8925
W www.
centralillustration.com

Guy Passey 237
Studio 503, Unit 3 Level 5
New England House
New England Street
Brighton
East Sussex BN1 4GH
T 01273 676 701
F 01273 676 701
M 07887 843 461
E guy.passey@virgin.net

Ali Pellatt 100
Unit 521
31 Clerkenwell Close
London EC1R 0AT
T 020 7490 4872
M 07932 726 725
E ali.pellatt@virgin.net
W www.cowboytime.co.uk

Simon Pemberton 47, 101
M 07976 625 802
W www.
simonpemberton.com
A Monster
Studio 32
10 Martello Street
London Fields E8 3PE
T 020 7923 9639
F 020 7923 9639
M 07790 986 670
E monsters@monsters.co.uk

Ingram Pinn 102
33 Alexandra Road
London W4 1AX
T 020 8994 5311
F 020 8747 8200
E ingram@
pinn33.freeserve.co.uk

Ian Pollock 103, 153
171 Bond Street
Macclesfield
Cheshire SK11 6RE
T 01625 426 205
F 01625 261 390
M 07770 927 940
E ianpllck@aol.com
W www.ianpollock.plus.com
A The Inkshed
98 Columbia Road
London E2 7QB
T 020 7613 2323
W www.inkshed.co.uk

Ashley Potter 47
the dairy
5-7 Marischal Road
London SE13 5LE
T 020 8297 2212
F 020 8297 1680
M 07930 492 471
E thedairy@btclick.com
W www.
thedairystudios.co.uk

Shelle Pugh 172
18 Rowley Hall Drive
Stafford ST17 9FF
T 01785 211 371
M 07941 054 090
E michelle.pugh@talk21.com

Shonagh Rae 104
T 020 7739 7765
M 07768 742 275
E big.orange@virgin.net

Finlay Ralph 173
4 Sandhurst Avenue
Withington
Manchester M20 1ED
M 07814 504 120
E finlay_ralph@hotmail.com
W www.dandad.org/gettyimagesbloodbank

Nik Ramage 104, 238-239
99A Newington Green Road
London N1 4QY
T 020 7354 8355
F 020 7359 5646
M 07976 314 302
E nik@nikramage.com
W www.nikramage.com

Darren Raven 105
15 Westgate Court
Canterbury Crescent
London SW9 7PR
T 020 7326 5042
F 020 7642 5704
M 07887 614 498
E darren@darrenraven.com
W www.darrenraven.com
A Three in a Box Inc
468 Queen Street East
104 Box 03
Toronto, M5A 1T7
Canada
T 020 8853 1236

Maria Raymondsdotter
22, 106, 107
c/o Stockholm Illustration
Stora Nygatan 44
S-11127 Stockholm
Sweden
T +46 8 224 010
F +46 8 5451 7115
M +46 70 491 8596
E maria@stockholmillustration.com
W www.raymondsdotter.com
A Central Illustration Agency
36 Wellington Street
London WC2E 7BD
T 020 7240 8925
W www.centralillustration.com

Chris Robson 108
13 Whatley Road
Clifton
Bristol BS8 2PS
T 0117 973 7694
M 07971 379 354
E chris@chrisrobson.com
W www.chrisrobson.com

Rachel Ross 153
A The Inkshed
98 Columbia Road
London E2 7QB
T 020 7613 2323
W www.inkshed.co.uk

Michael Sheehy 48, 240
115 Crystal Palace Road
East Dulwich
London SE22 9ES
T 020 8693 4315
F 020 8693 4315
E Michael.Sheehy@btinternet.com

Steve Shipley 173
112 Rigbourne Hill
Beccles
Suffolk NR34 9JH
T 01502 713 902
E steveshipley20@hotmail.com

Shin Shiraishi 241
Third Floor
29 Lithos Road
London NW3 6DX
T 020 7431 0958
F 020 7431 0958
M 07803 608 780
E shin@symbolonz.com
shin1shiraishi@hotmail.com
W www.symbolonz.com

Dionne Sievewright 241
Dunvegan
Wern-y-Cwrt
Near Raglan
Monmouthshire NP15 2JG
T 01291 690 158
F 01291 690 158
M 07778 150 110
E dionne@sievewright.freeserve.co.uk

Lasse Skarbovik 48, 242
A c/o Lorraine Owen
The Organisation
Basement
69 Caledonian Road
London N1 9BT
T 020 7833 8268
E organise@easynet.co.uk
W www.organisart.co.uk

Paul Slater 109
A Thorogood Illustration
5 Dryden Street
London WC2E 9NW
T 020 7829 8468
W www.thorogood.net

Andy Smith
23, 49, 110-111
A Private View Art Agency
8 North Hermitage
SY3 7JW
T 01743 350 355
E art@pvuk.com
W www.pvuk.com

Simon Spilsbury
24, 112, 243
36 Wellington Street
London WC2E 7BD
T 020 7836 1090
M 07885 629 597
E simon@spilsbury.co.uk

Julia Staite 174
27 Friars Walk
Southgate
London N14 5LR
M 07740 355 262
E jce_staite@hotmail.com

Karen Stannard 244
2 Wistlea Crescent
Colney Heath
St. Albans
Hertfordshire AL4 0NL
M 07790 351 444
E enq@karenstannard.co.uk
W www.karenstannard.co.uk

Tim Stevens 245
Walnut Tree House
63 Fornham Road
Bury St Edmunds
Suffolk IP32 6AW
T 01284 706 661
F 01284 706 661

David Tazzyman 25, 112
A Private View Art Agency
8 North Hermitage
SY3 7JW
T 01743 350 355
E art@pvuk.com
W www.pvuk.com

Michelle Thompson
50, 51, 246
M 07956 180 211
E michellethompson.studio@btinternet.com
W www.contact-me.net/MichelleThompson

Peter Till 113
11 Berkeley Road
London N8 8RU
T 020 8341 0497
F 020 8341 0497

Mike Todd 247
79 Eleanor Road
Waltham Cross
Hertfordshire EN8 7DW
T 01992 636 737
F 01992 636 737
E mike@oddballproductions.co.uk
W www.oddballproductions.co.uk

Nancy Tolford 114
20 Park Road
Walthamstow
London E17 7QF
T 020 8520 9204
F 020 8520 9204
M 07905 748 281
E ntolford@macunlimited.net
W www.nancytolford.com

Dominic Trevett 175
26 Windermere Avenue
London SW19 3ER
T 020 8540 0782
M 07779 447 676
E dominictrevett@hotmail.com
W www.illustratorbloke.com

Lucy Truman 156
28 Wilmot Street
Heanor
Derbyshire DE75 7EF
T 01773 714 754
01773 711 067 (Direct)
F 01773 711 067 (Direct)
M 07798 653 856
E lucytruman@lineone.net
A New Division
5 Risborough Street
London SE1 0HF
T 020 7593 0505
W www.newdivision.com

Bob Venables 26, 52, 115
109 Tuam Road
London SE18 2QY
T 020 8316 0223
F 020 8316 0223
M 07752 437 487
E robert.venables@virgin.net
A Thorogood Illustration
5 Dryden Street
London WC2E 9NW
T 020 7829 8468
W www.thorogood.net

Helen Wakefield 115-116
36 Ravenscroft
East Hunsbury
Northamptonshire NN4 0RL
T 01604 660 894
F 01604 660 894
M 07769 562 811

James Wakelin 176
99 Buckingham Road
Brighton
East Sussex BN1 3RB
M 07932 796 919
E jameswakelin@hotmail.com

Peter Warner 53
Peter Warner's Studio
Hillside Road
Tatsfield
Kent TN16 2NH
T 01959 577 270
F 01959 577 271
M 07958 531 538
E thestudio@peterwarner.com
W www.peterwarner.com

Paul Wearing
54, 117-119
PW Art Limited
Unit B4, Metropolitan Wharf
Wapping Wall
London E1W 3SS
T 020 7481 4653
F 020 7481 4654

Louise Weir 120
Studio 32
10 Martello Street
London Fields E8 3PE
T 020 7923 9639
M 07966 284 090
A Monster
Studio 32
10 Martello Street
London Fields E8 3PE
T 020 7923 9639

Ian Whadcock 28, 55, 121-123, 135, 154
T 01625 618 068
F 01625 618 129
E whadcock@mailbox.co.uk
A Eastwing
98 Columbia Road
London E2 7QB
T 020 7613 5580
W www.eastwing.co.uk

Bee Willey 137
A Illustration Ltd
1 Vicarage Crescent
London SW11 3LP
T 020 7228 8882
E team@illustrationweb.com
W www.mywholeportfolio.com/BeeWilley

Jonathan Williams
124, 248-249
M 07867 526 477
E jon@blazingfruit.com
W www.blazingfruit.com

Lu Willis 250-251
42 Courtlands
Maidenhead
Berkshire SL6 2PU
T/F 01628 623 327
M 07799 756 289

Adam Wilson 252
115 Norwich Road
Watton
Norfolk IP25 6DH
T 01953 884 345
E derangedofarkham@yahoo.co.uk
W www.adamwilson.info

Anne Wilson 138
A Illustration Ltd
1 Vicarage Crescent
London SW11 3LP
T 020 7228 8882
E team@illustrationweb.com
W www.mywholeportfolio.com/AnneWilson

Samantha Wilson
56, 124, 252
Glade House
32 The Common
Quarndon
Derby
Derbyshire DE22 5JY
T 01332 541 139
F 01332 550 495
M 07970 464 445
E sam.wil@virgin.net
A The Inkshed
98 Columbia Road
London E2 7QB
T 020 7613 2323
W www.inkshed.co.uk

Janet Woolley 124
A Arena
108 Leonard Street
London EC2A 4RH
T 020 7613 4040
E info@arenaworks.com
W www.arenaworks.com